Low cholesterol Cookbook for Beginners

Simple & Stress-free Low Carb Recipes Cookbook, 4 Weeks Meal Plan to Cut Cholesterol and Improve Heart Health

Naja V. Hansen

CONTENTS

Introduction 6

What Is Cholesterol? 6   LDL Cholesterol 8

HDL Cholesterol 7

Measurement Conversions 9

Breakfast And Brunch Recipes 12

Moroccan Lamb Kabobs 12   Good-morning Muffins 17

Spicy Omelet 12   Blueberry-banana Smoothie 17

Ciabatta Rolls 13   Egg White And Avocado Breakfast Wrap 18

Nutty Oat Cereal 13   Tempeh Caprese Breakfast Sandwiches 18

Oven-baked French Toast 14   Rolled Oats Cereal 19

Banana Oat Pancakes 14   Avocado And Kiwi Green Smoothies 19

Cashew & Berry Shake 15   Fruity Oatmeal Coffee Cake 20

Spinach Artichoke Pizza 15   Cranberry-orange Bread 20

Blueberry-walnut Muffins 16   Honey-wheat Sesame Bread 21

Orange-vanilla Smoothie 16   Carrot-oatmeal Bread 22

Poultry Recipes 24

Red Wine Chicken 24   Basil Chicken Meatballs 29

Chicken Stir-fry With Napa Cabbage 24   Crunchy Chicken Coleslaw Salad 29

Turkey Breast With Dried Fruit 25   Chicken Breasts With Mashed Beans 30

Turkey Tacos Verde 25   Balsamic Blueberry Chicken 31

Sesame-crusted Chicken 26   Turkey Curry With Fruit 31

Chicken Spicy Thai Style 26   Cashew Chicken 32

Hot-and-spicy Peanut Thighs 27   Nutty Coconut Chicken With Fruit Sauce 32

Chicken Pesto 27   Tandoori Turkey Pizzas 33

Mini Turkey Meatloaves 28   Chicken Breasts With Salsa 33

Mustard-roasted Almond Chicken Tenders 28   Sautéed Chicken With Roasted Garlic Sauce 34

Pork And Beef Mains Recipes 36

Spinach And Kale Salad With Spicy Pork 36   Beef And Avocado Quesadillas 39

Beef Rollups With Pesto 37   Chops With Mint And Garlic 40

Pork Quesadillas 37   Pork Goulash 40

Classic Spaghetti And Meatballs 38   Beef Burrito Skillet 41

Cowboy Steak With Chimichurri Sauce 38   Pork Scallops With Spinach 41

Pork Scallops Françoise 39   Sirloin Meatballs In Sauce 42

Lemon Basil Pork Medallions 42
Maple-balsamic Pork Chops 43
Sliced Flank Steak With Sherry-mustard Sauce 44
Cabbage Roll Sauté 44

Mustard And Thyme–crusted Beef Tenderloin 45
Pork Chops With Cabbage 45
Corned-beef Hash 46
Fiery Pork Stir-fry 47

Fish And Seafood Recipes 49

Grilled Scallops With Gremolata 49
Halibut Parcels 49
Cod Satay 50
Salmon With Farro Pilaf 51
Steamed Sole Rolls With Greens 51
Tilapia Mint Wraps 52
Halibut Burgers 52
Cod And Potatoes 53
Citrus Cod Bake 53
Catalán Salmon Tacos 54

Roasted Shrimp And Veggies 54
Sesame-pepper Salmon Kabobs 55
Cajun-rubbed Fish 56
Baked Halibut In Mustard Sauce 56
Seared Scallops With Fruit 57
Salmon With Spicy Mixed Beans 57
Scallops On Skewers With Lemon 58
Almond Snapper With Shrimp Sauce 58
Bluefish With Asian Seasonings 59
Red Snapper With Fruit Salsa 59

Vegetarian Mains Recipes 61

Homestyle Bean Soup 61
Peanut-butter-banana Skewered Sammies 61
Cheese-and-veggie Stuffed Artichokes 62
Roasted Garlic Soufflé 62
Spaghetti With Creamy Tomato Sauce 63
Salad Sandwich 63
Chili-sautéed Tofu With Almonds 64
Bean And Veggie Cassoulet 64
Rice-and-vegetable Casserole 65
Pinto Bean Tortillas 65

Quinoa-stuffed Peppers 66
Hearty Vegetable Stew 66
Spaghetti Sauce 67
Stuffed Noodle Squash 67
Quinoa Pepper Pilaf 68
Corn-and-chili Pancakes 68
Cauliflower, Green Pea, And Wild Rice Pilaf 69
Kidney Bean Stew 70
Sesame Soba Noodles 70
Pumpkin And Chickpea Patties 71

Soups, Salads, And Sides Recipes 73

Cosmoked Salmon And Turkey Wasabi Wraps 73
Fennel-and-orange Salad 73
Yogurt Cheese Balls 74
Piquant Navy Beans 74
butternut Squash And Lentil Soup 75
Lemony Green Beans With Almonds 75
Grilled Vegetable Pasta Salad 76
Roasted-garlic Corn 76
Rocket & Goat Cheese 77
Sautéed Fennel With Lemon 77

Beans For Soup 78
Greek Quesadillas 78
Tangy Fish And Tofu Soup 79
Scalloped Potatoes With Aromatic Vegetables 79
Sesame-roasted Vegetables 80
Legume Chili 80
Chunky Irish Potato-leek Soup 81
Low-sodium Chicken Broth 81
Chili Fries 82
Spring Asparagus Soup 82

Sauces, Dressings, And Staples Recipes 84

Fresh Lime Salsa 84
Silken Fruited Tofu Cream 84
Smoky Barbecue Rub 85
Chimichurri Rub 85
Double Tomato Sauce 86
Green Sauce 86
Zesty Citrus Kefir Dressing 87
Sun-dried Tomato And Kalamata Olive Tapenade 87
Chimichurri Sauce 88
Oregano-thyme Sauce 88

Tzatziki 88
Mustard Berry Vinaigrette 89
Tofu-horseradish Sauce 89
Cheesy Spinach Dip 90
Spicy Peanut Sauce 90
Classic Italian Tomato Sauce 91
Avocado Dressing 91
Spinach And Walnut Pesto 92
Lemon-garlic Sauce 92
Spicy Honey Sauce 92

Desserts And Treats Recipes 94

Banana-rum Mousse 94
Strawberry-apple-lemon Smoothie Pops 94
Peach Melba Frozen Yogurt Parfaits 95
Chocolate Granola Pie 95
Raisin Chocolate Slices 96
Loco Pie Crust 96
Cinnamon And Walnut Baked Pears 97
Mango Walnut Upside-down Cake 97
Choc Chip Banana Muffins 98
Sweet Potato And Chocolate Muffins 98

Loaded Soy Yogurt Bowls 99
Chocolate Chia Pudding 99
Luscious Mocha Mousse 100
Apple Cheesecake 100
Strawberry-mango Meringue Pie 101
Chocolate Mousse Banana Meringue Pie 101
Whole-wheat Chocolate Chip Cookies 102
Curried Fruit Compote 102
Chocolate, Peanut Butter, And Banana Ice Cream 103
Fudge Brownies 103

4-Week Meal Plan 104

APPENDIX : Recipes Index 106

Introduction

A high-cholesterol diagnosis does not mean you have to give up all the foods you love or spend hours in the kitchen cooking new dishes.

Yes, you will need to adopt a new approach to diet and exercise. That alone can feel intimidating at first—I know it was for me. But you can shift to a heart-healthy diet and exercise plan without it consuming every minute of your day.

Turns out, several well-known diets (DASH, Mediterranean) meet the nutritional guidelines for lowering cholesterol. They accomplish this by limiting saturated and trans fats, and emphasizing fruits, vegetables, whole grains, nuts, fiber, and low-fat proteins like fish and poultry. The fact that multiple popular diets can work to lower cholesterol is great in theory. But in practice, having to choose between several diet programs or figure out how to mix and match recipes can feel overwhelming.

Of course, changing habits is never easy. You will need to change your diet. Admittedly, you will need to limit (or cut out) red meat and full-fat dairy products and other foods high in saturated fat. Indeed, you will need to watch and limit your sodium and sugar intake. And you will need to exercise every day. But exercise can be as easy as a brisk 30-minute walk every day, and a heart-healthy diet really isn't that hard to achieve with the right support. Most importantly, it can work.

It's a change that can benefit everyone—from those already managing heart disease and taking a statin medication to those of us striving to lower cholesterol naturally. Choosing a cholesterol-lowering approach

to food and exercise can reduce your risk of heart disease.

Taking control and making a shift to a heart-healthy lifestyle can be empowering. Not only that, but it's exciting to discover healthy alternatives to your favorite foods, and find new, healthy, that are packed with flavor

What Is Cholesterol?

Cholesterol is a combination of two acetate molecules that join to form a waxy substance. It is found in animals because it's produced by the liver. Plants do not have any cholesterol. It is needed by the body to produce hormones and steroids and is used in the production of cell membranes. We need cholesterol to live.

But the amount of cholesterol in our bodies, and the balance between the two main types of cholesterol and other molecules like homocysteine, tri-glycerides, and free radicals, can predict whether we are at risk for diseases like atherosclerosis, heart disease, or stroke. Too much of the wrong kind of cholesterol can increase the risk of disease. And the way cholesterol interacts with other substances in the body increases disease risk, too.

Table 1-1

Cholesterol and Fat in Foods (Before Cooking)			
Food	**Total Fat**	**Saturated Fat**	**Cholesterol**
Chicken breast (4 ounces)	4.05 grams	1.15 grams	96.39 mg
Flank steak (4 ounces)	9.37 grams	3.89 grams	46.33 mg
Ground beef (4 ounces; 85 percent lean)	16.80 grams	6.57 grams	76.16 mg
Shrimp (4 ounces)	1.96 grams	0.37 grams	172.27 mg
Salmon (4 ounces)	12.30 grams	2.47 grams	66.87 mg
Ground turkey (4 ounces)	9.42 grams	2.56 grams	90.06 mg
Pork tenderloin (4 ounces)	6.14 grams	2.12 grams	74.84 mg
Olive oil (1 tablespoon)	13.50 grams	1.86 grams	0.0 mg
Almonds (¼ cup)	18.42 grams	1.42 grams	0.0 mg
Egg yolk (large)	4.51 grams	1.62 grams	209.78 mg

Cholesterol must combine with a protein and a fat in order to travel through the bloodstream. These combinations of molecules are called lipoproteins. There are two main types of lipoproteins: high-density and low-density (also known as HDL and LDL).

Total cholesterol levels of up to 200 mg/dL (milligrams per decaliter) are considered normal. Depending on your health and other risk factors, your doctor may want this level to be lower. If your level falls between 200 and 239 mg/dL, you'll want to evaluate your LDL/HDL ratio. The American Heart Association has different recommendations for tests and treatment depending on the combination of these factors.

Cholesterol levels will vary depending on your genet-ics, age, and even gender. The levels rise as we age. Men usually have higher levels than premeno-pausal women, but after menopause women's cholesterol counts increase.

HDL Cholesterol

HDL, or high density lipoprotein, is known as the "good" cholesterol because it removes LDL cholester-ol from the bloodstream and takes it to the liver to be metabolized into bile salts and excreted. This type of cholesterol may actually scour your arteries, helping remove LDL cholesterol and reducing atherosclerosis and plaque formation. Here are some foods that in-crease HDL levels:

- Olive oil
- Nuts
- Avocados
- Peanut butter
- High-fiber foods
- Moderate alcohol consumption
- Dried beans
- Whole grains
- Citrus fruits
- Dark chocolate

- Oatmeal and oat bran
- Orange juice
- Apples
- Walnuts and almonds
- Flaxseed
- Fatty fish
- Legumes
- Barley
- Cherries
- Vegetables

For a healthy body, your HDL cholesterol levels should be above 40 mg/dL. Fortunately, your diet and lifestyle, including the right foods and exercise, can have a significant impact on HDL levels.

LDL Cholesterol

LDL, or low density lipoprotein, is known as the "bad" cholesterol because it transports cholesterol from the liver to the bloodstream. Research indicates that plaque, which can form on arterial walls and narrow the arteries, may be filled with LDL cholesterol. Here are some foods that reduce LDL levels:

Your LDL cholesterol levels should be less than 100 mg/dL. Over 160 mg/dL is considered high. The level of this type of cholesterol responds well to changes in diet and the addition of exercise.

The Total/HDL Cholesterol Proportion

The proportion of total cholesterol to HDL in your blood is an important risk predictor for heart disease. To calculate this, divide your total cholesterol level by your HDL level. The ratio you want to reach is below 3.5 to 1. Anything about 5 to 1 or higher indicates an increased risk of heart disease.

Breakfast And Brunch Recipes

Breakfast And Brunch Recipes

Moroccan Lamb Kabobs

Servings: 6
Ingredients:
- ¼ cup olive oil
- ½ cup chopped fresh mint
- 4 cloves garlic, minced
- ½ teaspoon ground cardamom
- ½ teaspoon cinnamon
- ¼ teaspoon pepper
- 3 tablespoons orange juice
- 1 pound lean lamb
- 1 (8-ounce) package button mushrooms
- 2 red bell peppers, sliced

Directions:
1. In glass bowl, combine oil, mint, garlic, cardamom, cinnamon, pepper, and orange juice and mix well. Trim fat from lamb and cut into 1″ cubes. Add to marinade, cover, and refrigerate for 2–4 hours.
2. When ready to eat, preheat broiler. Drain lamb, reserving marinade. Thread lamb, mushrooms, and peppers on metal skewers.
3. Broil skewers 6″ from heat source, turning several times during cooking and brushing with reserved marinade, for 7–9 minutes or until lamb is browned and just pink inside. Discard remaining marinade. Serve immediately.

Nutrition Info:
- Per Serving: Calories: 167.27; Fat:7.40 g ;Saturated fat: 2.10 g ;Sodium:53.38 mg

Spicy Omelet

Servings: 2
Cooking Time: 8 Minutes
Ingredients:
- 1 whole egg
- 6 egg whites
- 1 tablespoon water
- ¼ teaspoon chili powder
- Pinch salt
- ⅛ teaspoon white pepper
- Olive oil cooking spray
- ½ cup salsa
- 1 cup arugula or baby spinach leaves

Directions:
1. In a medium bowl, combine the egg, egg whites, water, chili powder, salt, and white pepper, and beat well with a fork.
2. Spray an 8-inch omelet pan or nonstick skillet with olive oil cooking spray, and heat over medium heat.
3. When a drop of water in the pan skitters, add the egg mixture. Cook over medium heat, shaking the pan occasionally, lifting the edges of the omelet with a nonstick spatula so uncooked egg can flow underneath, and running the spatula

around the edge of the pan to make sure the omelet isn't sticking.

4. When the eggs are set but still moist on top, spread the salsa and the arugula or baby spinach evenly across one half. Fold the omelet in half and slide onto a warmed plate. Cut in half and serve immediately.

Nutrition Info:
- Per Serving: Calories: 109 ; Fat: 3 g ;Saturated fat: 1 g ;Sodium: 594 mg

Ciabatta Rolls

Servings: 6
Ingredients:
- 1 recipe Whole-Grain Ciabatta
- 2 tablespoons olive oil
- 3 tablespoons cornmeal

Directions:
1. Prepare Ciabatta through the first rising. Punch down dough and turn onto lightly floured surface.
2. Divide dough into 6 portions. Using floured fingers, shape each portion into a 3″ × 3″ rectangle. Grease six 4″ × 4″ squares on a cookie sheet with olive oil and sprinkle with cornmeal. Place dough onto each cornmeal coated square. Drizzle with remaining olive oil.
3. Let rise in warm place until doubled in size, about 45 minutes. Preheat oven to 425ºF. Bake rolls for 10–15 minutes or until very light brown. Turn off oven and prop open oven door. Let rolls stand in oven for another 5 minutes. Then remove from oven and let cool on wire racks.

Nutrition Info:
- Per Serving: Calories:283.00 ; Fat: 6.17 g ;Saturated fat:0.91 g ;Sodium: 203.58 mg

Nutty Oat Cereal

Servings: 4
Cooking Time: 30 Min
Ingredients:
- Parchment paper
- 1 cup rolled oats
- 1 cup dried pumpkin seeds
- ½ cup unsalted mixed nuts, roughly chopped
- Pinch fine sea salt
- 1 tbsp. olive oil
- 2 cups unsweetened cashew milk
- 1 cup strawberries, chopped
- 1 cup blueberries

Directions:
1. Heat the oven to 300°F gas mark 2. Line a baking sheet with parchment paper.
2. In a medium-sized mixing bowl, add the oats, pumpkin seeds, mixed nuts, salt, and olive oil, mix to combine.
3. Transfer the oat mixture onto the prepared baking sheet in a thin layer.
4. Bake for 30 minutes, mixing the oats halfway through cooking, until lightly browned. Remove and set aside to cool.
5. Serve with cashew milk, chopped strawberries, and blueberries.

Nutrition Info:
- Per Serving: Calories: 460 ; Fat: 32g ;Saturated fat: 3 g ;Sodium: 106 mg

Oven-baked French Toast

Servings: 4
Cooking Time: 30 Minutes
Ingredients:
- Olive oil
- 8 slices whole wheat bread
- 3 eggs
- 1 cup low-fat milk
- 1 tablespoon maple syrup
- 1 teaspoon cinnamon

Directions:
1. Preheat the oven to 350°F. Lightly grease 9-by-5-inch baking pan with olive oil.
2. Cut the bread into ½-inch squares and place them into the baking pan.
3. In a medium bowl, whisk together the eggs, milk, maple syrup, and cinnamon.
4. Pour the egg mixture over the bread, ensuring all the bread is well coated.
5. Bake for 30 minutes. Serve immediately.

Nutrition Info:
- Per Serving: Calories: 285 ; Fat: 2 g ;Saturated fat: 2 g ;Sodium: 372 mg

Banana Oat Pancakes

Servings: 7
Cooking Time: 20 Minutes
Ingredients:
- 1 cup steel-cut oats
- 1 banana
- 1 large egg
- ½ cup low-fat milk (or plant-based alternative)
- 2 teaspoons baking powder
- Olive oil

Directions:
1. In a blender, place the oats, banana, egg, milk, and baking powder and blend until smooth, about 20 seconds.
2. Place a medium skillet over medium heat and coat it with olive oil.
3. Using ¼-cup measurements, add the batter to the hot skillet to form 4 pancakes.
4. Cook the pancakes until the edges turn slightly golden, about 2 minutes. Then flip them and cook for another 2 minutes on the other side. Remove the pancakes from the skillet and repeat with the remaining batter. Serve immediately.

Nutrition Info:
- Per Serving: Calories: 143 ; Fat: 3g ;Saturated fat: 1g ;Sodium: 19 mg

Cashew & Berry Shake

Servings: 2
Cooking Time: 5 Min
Ingredients:

- 2 cups fresh or frozen berries (your choice)
- 1¾ cups unsweetened cashew milk
- 1 cup fresh or frozen spinach, roughly chopped
- ¼ cup cashew butter
- ½ cup ice cubes

Directions:

1. In a blender, add the berries of choice, cashew milk, spinach, and cashew butter. Blend until lump-free and smooth.
2. Add the ice cubes and blend until smooth.

Nutrition Info:

- Per Serving: Calories: 324 ; Fat: 22g ;Saturated fat: 1 g ;Sodium: 186 mg

Spinach Artichoke Pizza

Servings: 8
Ingredients:

- 1 (10-ounce) package frozen chopped spinach, thawed and drained
- 1 (9-ounce) package frozen artichoke hearts, thawed and drained
- 1 tablespoon olive oil
- 1 onion, chopped
- 3 cloves garlic, minced
- 1 red bell pepper, chopped
- 1 (8-ounce) package sliced mushrooms
- 1 cup part-skim ricotta cheese
- ¼ cup grated Parmesan cheese
- 1 cup shredded part-skim mozzarella cheese
- ½ cup shredded extra-sharp Cheddar cheese
- 1 Whole-Grain Pizza Crust

Directions:

1. Preheat oven to 400ºF. Press spinach between paper towels to remove all excess moisture. Cut artichoke hearts into small pieces.
2. In large saucepan, heat olive oil. Cook onion, garlic, red pepper, and mushrooms until crisp-tender, about 4 minutes. Add spinach; cook and stir until liquid evaporates, about 5 minutes longer. Add mushrooms; cook and stir for 2–3 minutes longer.
3. Drain vegetable mixture if necessary. Place in medium bowl and let cool for 20 minutes. Then blend in ricotta and Parmesan cheeses.
4. Spread on pizza crust. Top with mozzarella and Cheddar cheeses. Bake for 20–25 minutes or until pizza is hot and cheese is melted and begins to brown. Serve immediately.

Nutrition Info:

- Per Serving: Calories: 335.56; Fat:13.05 g ;Saturated fat: 6.06 g ;Sodium: 317.04 mg

Blueberry-walnut Muffins

Servings: 12

Ingredients:

- 1 cup buttermilk
- 1 egg
- 2 egg whites
- 6 tablespoons canola oil
- ½ cup sugar
- 1/8 teaspoon salt
- 1¼ cups all-purpose flour
- ¼ cup whole-wheat flour
- 1 teaspoon baking powder
- 1 teaspoon baking soda
- 1 cup blueberries
- 1 tablespoon flour
- ½ cup chopped walnuts
- 2 tablespoons brown sugar
- ½ teaspoon cinnamon

Directions:

1. Preheat oven to 400ºF. Line 12 muffin cups with paper liners and set aside. In large bowl, combine buttermilk, egg, egg whites, oil, sugar, and salt and mix well.
2. Stir in 1¼ cups flour, whole-wheat flour, baking powder, and baking soda just until dry ingredients are moistened. In small bowl, toss blueberries with 1 tablespoon flour. Stir into batter along with walnuts.
3. Fill prepared muffin cups ¼ full. In small bowl, combine 2 tablespoons brown sugar and cinnamon and sprinkle over muffins. Bake for 17–22 minutes or until golden-brown and set. Remove from muffin cups and cool on wire racks.

Nutrition Info:

- Per Serving: Calories: 230.36; Fat:10.80 g ;Saturated fat:0.95 g ;Sodium: 197.52 mg

Orange-vanilla Smoothie

Servings: 2

Ingredients:

- 1½ cups orange yogurt
- ½ cup orange juice
- 1 orange, peeled and sliced
- ¼ cup vanilla-flavored whey protein
- 1 teaspoon vanilla
- 4 ice cubes

Directions:

1. Place yogurt, orange juice, orange, whey protein, and vanilla in blender or food processor; blend or process until smooth. Add ice cubes; blend or process until thick. Pour into glasses and serve immediately.

Nutrition Info:

- Per Serving: Calories: 346.91; Fat: 2.34 g ;Saturated fat: 1.22 gr;Sodium: 241.12 mg

Good-morning Muffins

Servings: 18

Ingredients:

- 1 cup all-purpose flour
- 1 cup whole-wheat flour
- 2 tablespoons oat bran
- 2 tablespoons ground flaxseed
- ½ cup brown sugar
- ½ cup sugar
- 2 teaspoons cinnamon
- ¼ teaspoon nutmeg
- 1½ teaspoons baking powder
- 1 teaspoon baking soda
- 2 apples, peeled and chopped
- 1 cup grated carrots
- ½ cup applesauce
- 1 egg
- 1 egg white
- ¼ cup low-fat sour cream
- ¼ cup canola oil
- 2 teaspoons vanilla
- 1 cup dried cranberries
- 1 cup chopped walnuts

Directions:

1. Preheat oven to 375ºF. Line 18 muffin cups with paper liners and set aside. In large bowl, combine flour, whole-wheat flour, oat bran, flaxseed, sugar, brown sugar, cinnamon, nutmeg, baking powder, and baking soda and mix well.
2. In medium bowl, combine apples, carrots, applesauce, egg, egg white, sour cream, canola oil, and vanilla, and beat to combine. Add to flour mixture and stir just until dry ingredients are moistened. Fold in cranberries and walnuts.
3. Fill prepared muffin cups ¼ full. Bake for 15–25 minutes, or until muffins are golden-brown and toothpick inserted in center comes out clean. Remove from muffin cups and cool on wire rack.

Nutrition Info:

- Per Serving: Calories: 210.22; Fat:8.48 g ;Saturated fat:0.86 g ;Sodium:116.29 mg

Blueberry-banana Smoothie

Servings: 2

Ingredients:

- 1½ cups skim milk
- 1 banana
- 1 cup blueberries
- 1 cup nonfat vanilla yogurt
- 4 ice cubes

Directions:

1. Place milk, banana, blueberries, and yogurt in blender or food processor; blend or process until smooth. Add ice cubes; blend or process until thick. Pour into glasses and serve immediately.

Nutrition Info:

- Per Serving: Calories:283.52 ; Fat:4.83 g ;Saturated fat: 2.77 g;Sodium: 159.60 mg

Egg White And Avocado Breakfast Wrap

Servings: 1
Cooking Time: 6 Minutes
Ingredients:

- 2 teaspoons olive oil
- ½ red pepper, seeded and sliced
- ½ cup liquid egg whites
- ¼ avocado, pitted and sliced
- 2 tablespoons Fresh Lime Salsa
- 1 (6½-inch) whole wheat tortilla (or pita)

Directions:

1. In a medium skillet, heat the olive oil over medium-high heat. Add the red pepper and cook for 3 minutes until slightly soft, then remove and set aside.
2. In the same skillet over medium-high heat, scramble the egg whites until cooked through and no longer runny, about 3 minutes, then remove from heat.
3. Spread the scrambled eggs, cooked red peppers, avocado, and Fresh Lime Salsa over the tortilla.
4. Wrap up the tortilla and serve immediately.

Nutrition Info:

- Per Serving: Calories:407 ; Fat: 21g ;Saturated fat: 5g ;Sodium: 488mg

Tempeh Caprese Breakfast Sandwiches

Servings: X
Cooking Time: 10 Minutes
Ingredients:

- 4 slices dark rye bread
- 3 teaspoons olive oil, divided
- 6 ounces tempeh, cut into 2 slices
- 1 large tomato, thinly sliced
- ¼ cup shredded fresh basil
- ½ cup fat-free shredded mozzarella
- Sea salt
- Freshly ground black pepper

Directions:

1. Preheat the oven to 400°F. Line a baking sheet with parchment paper.
2. Brush both sides of each bread slice with 2 teaspoons olive oil and arrange the bread on the baking sheet. Toast the bread in the oven until lightly browned and crispy, turning once, about 4 minutes.
3. In a medium skillet, warm the remaining 1 teaspoon olive oil over medium heat. Panfry the tempeh until it is browned and crispy, turning once, about 6 minutes.
4. Remove the bread from the oven and remove the tempeh from the heat.
5. Place two slices of bread on a cutting board and top with the tempeh slices. Evenly divide the tomato slices, basil, and cheese onto the tempeh. Season with salt and pepper.
6. Top with the remaining slices of bread and cut the sandwiches in half diagonally. Serve.

Nutrition Info:

- Per Serving: Calories: 464 ; Fat: 19 g ;Saturated fat: 3 g ;Sodium: 237 mg

Rolled Oats Cereal

Servings: 4
Cooking Time: 5 Min
Ingredients:
- 2 tbsp. plant-based butter, plus 1 tablespoon unsalted butter
- 1 tbsp. organic honey
- ¾ cup rolled oats
- ⅓ cup walnuts, roughly chopped
- 1 tbsp. chia seeds
- 1 tbsp. hemp seeds
- 1 tbsp. ground flaxseed
- ½ tsp ground cinnamon
- Pinch fine sea salt
- 2 tbsp. dried cranberries
- 2 tbsp. raisins

Directions:
1. In a large heavy bottom pan, melt the butter and honey over medium heat, cook until bubbly.
2. Mix in the oats, walnuts, chia seeds, hemp seeds, flaxseed, cinnamon, and salt. Cook for 3 to 4 minutes, stirring until the oats and nuts start to brown. If the mixture is browning too fast, turn the heat down to low. Remove from the heat and add the cranberries and raisins, mix to combine.
3. Eat the oat cereal right away or cool it completely, then store it in an airtight container.

Nutrition Info:
- Per Serving: Calories: 230 ; Fat: 16 g ;Saturated fat: 3 g ;Sodium: 64 mg

Avocado And Kiwi Green Smoothies

Servings: X
Ingredients:
- 1 cup unsweetened apple juice
- 1 avocado, cubed
- 1 cup roughly chopped kale
- 1 kiwi, peeled and chopped
- ½ cup coconut water or water
- 2 tablespoons honey
- 1 tablespoon chopped fresh basil
- 1 tablespoon chopped fresh mint

Directions:
1. In a blender, add the apple juice, avocado, kale, kiwi, coconut water, honey, basil, and mint and blend until very smooth.
2. Pour into glasses and serve immediately.

Nutrition Info:
- Per Serving: Calories: 308 ; Fat:14 g ;Saturated fat: 2 g ;Sodium: 28 mg

Fruity Oatmeal Coffee Cake

Servings: 16
Ingredients:

- ½ cup brown sugar
- 1½ teaspoons cinnamon
- 1 cup oatmeal
- ½ cup chopped walnuts
- 6 tablespoons canola oil, divided
- 2 tablespoons butter or plant sterol margarine
- 1 cup blueberries
- ½ cup dried cranberries
- 1 egg
- 2 egg whites
- ¼ cup buttermilk
- ¼ cup orange juice
- 2/3 cup sugar
- 1 cup all-purpose flour
- 1 cup whole-wheat flour
- 2 teaspoons baking powder
- 1 teaspoon baking soda

Directions:

1. Preheat oven to 350ºF. Spray a 13″ × 9″ baking pan with nonstick cooking spray containing flour, and set aside.
2. In medium bowl, combine brown sugar, cinnamon, oatmeal, and walnuts and mix well. In small saucepan, melt together 2 tablespoons canola oil and the butter. Pour into oatmeal mixture and stir until crumbs form. Add blueberries and cranberries; set aside.
3. In large bowl, combine remaining 4 tablespoons oil, egg, egg whites, buttermilk, orange juice, and sugar and beat until combined. Add flour, whole-wheat flour, baking powder, and baking soda and stir just until dry ingredients are moistened.
4. Spoon and spread batter into prepared pan. Evenly sprinkle oatmeal mixture over the batter. Bake for 30–40 minutes or until coffee cake is golden-brown and toothpick inserted in center comes out clean. Serve warm.

Nutrition Info:

- Per Serving: Calories: 261.93 ; Fat:10.24 g ;Saturated fat: 1.72 g;Sodium: 161.27 mg

Cranberry-orange Bread

Servings: 12
Ingredients:

- ¼ cup orange juice
- 2 tablespoons frozen orange juice concentrate, thawed
- ½ teaspoon almond extract
- ¼ cup canola oil
- 1 egg
- 1/3 cup sugar
- ½ cup brown sugar
- 1 teaspoon grated orange zest
- 1½ cups all-purpose flour
- ¼ cup whole-wheat flour
- 1 teaspoon baking soda
- 1 teaspoon baking powder
- 2 cups chopped cranberries

- ½ cup chopped hazelnuts

Directions:
1. Preheat oven to 350°F. Spray a 9″ × 5″ loaf pan with nonstick cooking spray containing flour, and set aside.
2. In medium bowl, combine orange juice, orange juice concentrate, almond extract, canola oil, egg, sugar, brown sugar, and orange zest and beat to combine.
3. In large bowl, combine flour, whole-wheat flour, baking soda, baking powder, and mix. Make a well in the center of the flour mixture and pour in the orange juice mixture. Stir just until dry ingredients are moistened.
4. Fold in cranberries and hazelnuts. Pour into prepared pan. Bake for 55–65 minutes or until bread is golden-brown and toothpick inserted in center comes out clean. Remove from pan and let cool on wire rack.

Nutrition Info:
- Per Serving: Calories: 232.48; Fat: 8.24 g ;Saturated fat:0.72g ;Sodium: 145.81 mg

Honey-wheat Sesame Bread

Servings: 32
Ingredients:
- 1 cup milk
- 1 cup water
- ½ cup honey
- 3 tablespoons butter
- ¼ teaspoon salt
- 1 egg
- 2 cups whole-wheat flour
- 2 (¼-ounce) packages instant-blend dry yeast
- ½ cup sesame seeds
- 3 to 4 cups all-purpose flour
- 1 egg white
- 2 tablespoons sesame seeds

Directions:
1. In medium saucepan, combine milk, water, honey, butter, and salt. Heat over medium heat until butter melts. Remove from heat and let stand for 30 minutes or until just lukewarm. Beat in egg.
2. Meanwhile, in large bowl combine whole-wheat flour, instant-blend yeast, and ½ cup sesame seeds. Add milk mixture and beat for 1 minute. Then gradually stir in enough all-purpose flour to make a firm dough.
3. Turn out onto floured surface and knead, adding additional flour if necessary, until dough is elastic. Place in greased bowl, turning to grease top; cover and let rise until double, about 1 hour.
4. Grease two 9″ × 5″ loaf pans with unsalted butter and set aside. Punch down dough and divide into two parts. On floured surface, roll or pat to 7″ × 12″ rectangle. Roll up tightly, starting with 7″ side. Place in prepared pans. Brush with egg white and sprinkle each with 1 tablespoon sesame seeds.
5. Cover with towel, and let rise until double, about 30 minutes. Preheat oven to 350°F. Bake loaves for 35–45 minutes or until golden brown. Turn onto wire rack to cool completely.

Nutrition Info:
- Per Serving: Calories: 131.38; Fat: 3.02 g ;Saturated fat: 1.03 g ;Sodium: 34.51 mg

Servings: 12

Ingredients:

- 1½ cups finely chopped carrots
- 1 cup water
- 1½ cups all-purpose flour
- ¼ cup oatmeal
- 2 tablespoons oat bran
- ½ cup brown sugar
- 1/3 cup sugar
- ½ teaspoon salt
- 1 teaspoon baking powder
- ½ teaspoon baking soda
- ½ teaspoon cinnamon
- ½ teaspoon ginger
- 2/3 cup applesauce
- ¼ cup canola oil
- 2 egg whites
- ½ cup chopped walnuts

Directions:

1. Preheat oven to 350ºF. Spray a 9″ × 5″ loaf pan with nonstick cooking spray containing flour, and set aside.
2. In small saucepan, combine carrots and water and bring to a boil. Reduce heat and simmer for 5–7 minutes or until carrots are tender. Drain carrots and mash until smooth. Set aside.
3. In large bowl, combine flour, oatmeal, oat bran, brown sugar, sugar, salt, baking powder, baking soda, cinnamon, and ginger and mix well. In medium bowl combine mashed carrots, applesauce, canola oil, and egg whites, and beat well. Stir into dry ingredients until blended. Fold in walnuts.
4. Pour batter into prepared pan. Bake for 55–65 minutes or until bread is deep golden-brown and toothpick inserted in center comes out clean. Remove from pan and let cool on wire rack.

Nutrition Info:

- Per Serving: Calories: 241.05; Fat: 8.56 g ;Saturated fat:0.66 g ;Sodium:107.36 mg

Poultry Recipes

Poultry Recipes

Red Wine Chicken

Servings: 4
Cooking Time: 30 Min
Ingredients:
- 2 tbsp. plant-based butter, plus 1 tbsp. olive oil
- 1 lb. boneless, skinless chicken thighs
- ¼ tsp fine sea salt
- Ground black pepper
- 3 large carrots, peeled and thinly sliced
- 8 oz button mushrooms, sliced
- 1 small brown onion, sliced
- 1 cup Pinot Noir red wine
- 1 cup low-sodium chicken stock
- 1 tbsp. tomato paste
- 3 rosemary sprigs

Directions:
1. Melt the butter in a large, heavy-bottom pan over medium-high heat. Sprinkle the chicken thighs with salt and pepper.
2. Once the butter starts to froth, add the chicken thighs, and brown for 1 to 2 minutes on each side. Transfer to a plate.
3. Add the carrots, mushrooms, and onion to the pan. Fry for 3 to 4 minutes, until the onion starts to soften. Add the red wine, chicken stock, tomato paste, and rosemary sprigs. Cook for 7 to 8 minutes, until the vegetables are tender.
4. Return the chicken thighs to the pan, and simmer for 5 to 10 minutes, until cooked through. Remove the rosemary sprigs and serve.

Nutrition Info:
- Per Serving: Calories: 296 ; Fat:12 g ;Saturated fat: 3 g ;Sodium: 115 mg

Chicken Stir-fry With Napa Cabbage

Servings: 4
Ingredients:
- 2 (5-ounce) boneless, skinless chicken breasts
- 2 tablespoons cornstarch
- 2 tablespoons lemon juice
- 1 tablespoon low-sodium soy sauce
- 1 cup Low-Sodium Chicken Broth
- 2 tablespoons peanut oil
- 4 cups shredded Napa cabbage
- 4 green onions, sliced
- 1 green bell pepper, sliced
- 1½ cups frozen edamame, thawed

Directions:
1. Cut chicken into 1″ pieces. In small bowl, combine cornstarch, lemon juice, soy sauce, and chicken broth. Add chicken and let stand for 15 minutes.
2. Heat oil in large skillet or wok. Drain chicken, reserving marinade. Add chicken to skillet; stir-fry until almost cooked, about 4 minutes. Remove chicken to a plate.

3. Add cabbage and green onions to skillet; stir fry until cabbage wilts, about 4 minutes. Add bell pepper and edamame; stir-fry for 3–5 minutes longer until hot.
4. Stir marinade and add to skillet along with chicken. Stir-fry until sauce bubbles and thickens and chicken is thoroughly cooked. Serve over hot cooked brown rice.

Nutrition Info:
* Per Serving: Calories:307.21; Fat: 14.90 g ;Saturated fat: 2.47 g ;Sodium:214.61 mg

Turkey Breast With Dried Fruit

Servings: 6
Ingredients:
* 1½ pounds bone-in turkey breast
* 1/8 teaspoon salt
* 1/8 teaspoon pepper
* 1 tablespoon flour
* 1 tablespoon olive oil
* 1 tablespoon butter or plant sterol margarine
* ½ cup chopped prunes
* ½ cup chopped dried apricots
* 2 Granny Smith apples, peeled and chopped
* 1 cup Low-Sodium Chicken Broth
* ¼ cup Madeira wine

Directions:
1. Sprinkle turkey with salt, pepper, and flour. In large saucepan, heat olive oil and butter over medium heat. Add turkey and cook until browned, about 5 minutes. Turn turkey.
2. Add all fruit to saucepan along with broth and wine. Cover and bring to a simmer. Reduce heat to medium low and simmer for 55–65 minutes or until turkey is thoroughly cooked. Serve turkey with fruit and sauce.

Nutrition Info:
* Per Serving: Calories: 293.15; Fat: 6.01 g   ;Saturated fat: 1.94 g ;Sodium: 127.28 mg

Turkey Tacos Verde

Servings: 4
Cooking Time: 13 Minutes
Ingredients:
* 1 teaspoon olive oil
* 1 pound 99% lean ground white turkey
* 1 onion, chopped
* 3 cloves garlic, minced
* 10 tomatillos, husk removed, rinsed and chopped
* 2 jalapeño peppers, seeded and minced
* ½ cup low-sodium salsa verde
* 8 corn tortillas, warmed
* ½ cup low-fat plain Greek yogurt
* 2 tablespoons chopped fresh cilantro
* 2 scallions, minced
* 2 cups mixed salad greens

Directions:
1. In a large nonstick skillet, heat the olive oil over medium heat.
2. Add the ground turkey, onion, and garlic and stir to break up the meat.

3. Sauté the mixture until the turkey is cooked through, about 5 to 6 minutes.
4. Add the tomatillos and jalapeño peppers and stir for 3 to 4 minutes. Then add the salsa verde and stir.
5. Meanwhile, combine the yogurt, cilantro, and scallions in a small bowl
6. Assemble the tacos starting with the tortillas, turkey mixture, yogurt mixture, and top with the salad greens. Serve immediately.

Nutrition Info:
- Per Serving: Calories:338 ; Fat : 6 g ;Saturated fat: 1 g ;Sodium: 295 mg

Sesame-crusted Chicken

Servings: 4
Ingredients:
- 2 tablespoons low-sodium soy sauce
- 2 cloves garlic, minced
- 1 tablespoon grated ginger root
- 1 tablespoon brown sugar
- 1 teaspoon sesame oil
- 4 (4-ounce) boneless, skinless chicken breasts
- ½ cup sesame seeds
- 3 tablespoons olive oil
- 1 tablespoon butter

Directions:
1. In large food storage heavy-duty plastic bag, combine soy sauce, garlic, ginger root, brown sugar, and sesame oil and mix well. Add chicken; seal bag, and squish to coat chicken with marinade. Place in bowl and refrigerate for 8 hours.
2. When ready to eat, remove chicken from marinade; discard marinade. Dip chicken in sesame seeds to coat on all sides.
3. Heat olive oil and butter in large skillet over medium heat. Add chicken and cook for 5 minutes. Carefully turn chicken and cook for 3–6 minutes on second side or until chicken is thoroughly cooked and sesame seeds are toasted. Serve immediately.

Nutrition Info:
- Per Serving: Calories: 363.65; Fat: 20.83 g ;Saturated fat:4.15 g;Sodium: 250.28 mg

Chicken Spicy Thai Style

Servings: 4
Ingredients:
- 2 tablespoons lime juice
- 1 tablespoon low-sodium soy sauce
- ½ cup Low-Sodium Chicken Broth
- ¼ cup dry white wine
- ¼ cup natural peanut butter
- 2 tablespoons peanut oil
- 1 onion, chopped
- 4 cloves garlic, minced
- 3 (4-ounce) boneless, skinless chicken breasts, sliced
- 4 cups shredded Napa cabbage
- 1 cup shredded carrots

Directions:
1. In small bowl, combine lime juice, soy sauce, chicken broth, wine, and peanut butter and mix with wire whisk until blended. Set aside.

2. In wok or large skillet, heat peanut oil over medium-high heat. Add onion and garlic; stir-fry until crisp-tender, about 4 minutes. Add chicken; stir-fry until almost cooked, about 3 minutes. Add cabbage and carrots; stir-fry until cabbage begins to wilt, about 3–4 minutes longer.
3. Remove food from wok and return wok to heat. Add peanut butter mixture and bring to a simmer. Return chicken and vegetables to wok; stir fry until sauce bubbles and thickens and chicken is thoroughly cooked, about 3–4 minutes. Serve immediately.

Nutrition Info:
- Per Serving: Calories: 300.35; Fat:16.70 g ;Saturated fat:3.20 g;Sodium:309.32 mg

Hot-and-spicy Peanut Thighs

Servings: 4
Ingredients:
- 4 (4-ounce) chicken thighs
- ½ cup low-sodium barbecue sauce
- 2 teaspoons chili powder
- ½ cup chopped unsalted peanuts

Directions:
1. Preheat oven to 350ºF. Spray a roasting pan with nonstick cooking spray and set aside. Pound chicken slightly, to " thickness.
2. In shallow bowl, combine barbecue sauce and chili powder and mix well. Dip chicken into sauce, then dip one side into peanuts. Place, peanut side up, in prepared pan.
3. Bake for 30–40 minutes, or until chicken is thoroughly cooked and nuts are browned. Serve immediately.

Nutrition Info:
- Per Serving: Calories: 327.41; Fat: 19.55 g ;Saturated fat: 4.22 g;Sodium: 129.88 mg

Chicken Pesto

Servings: 6
Ingredients:
- 1 cup packed fresh basil leaves
- ¼ cup toasted chopped hazelnuts
- 2 cloves garlic, chopped
- 2 tablespoons olive oil
- 1 tablespoons water
- ¼ cup grated Parmesan cheese
- ½ cup Low-Sodium Chicken Broth
- 12 ounces boneless, skinless chicken breasts
- 1 (12-ounce) package angel hair pasta

Directions:
1. Bring a large pot of salted water to a boil. In blender or food processor, combine basil, hazelnuts, and garlic. Blend or process until very finely chopped. Add olive oil and water; blend until a paste forms. Then blend in Parmesan cheese; set aside.
2. In large skillet, bring chicken broth to a simmer over medium heat. Cut chicken into strips and add to broth. Cook for 4 minutes, then add the pasta to the boiling water.
3. Cook pasta for 3–4 minutes according to package directions, until al dente. Drain and add to chicken mixture; cook and stir for 1 minute until chicken is thoroughly cooked. Add basil mixture, remove from heat, and stir until a sauce forms. Serve immediately.

Nutrition Info:
- Per Serving: Calories: 373.68; Fat: 11.06 g ;Saturated fat: 2.01 g ;Sodium: 108.92 mg

Mini Turkey Meatloaves

Servings: 4
Cooking Time: 20 Minutes
Ingredients:

- ⅓ cup old-fashioned rolled oats
- 2 scallions, finely chopped
- 1 egg
- 3 tablespoons no-salt-added tomato paste, divided
- 2 teaspoons olive oil
- Pinch salt
- ⅛ teaspoon black pepper
- ½ teaspoon dried ground leaves
- 16 ounces 99% lean ground white turkey
- 2 tablespoons low-sodium mustard
- 1 tablespoon water

Directions:

1. Preheat the oven to 450°F. Line a baking sheet with aluminum foil.
2. In a large bowl, combine the oats, scallions, egg, 2 tablespoons of the tomato paste, olive oil, salt, pepper, and marjoram, and mix well.
3. Add the ground turkey, and mix gently with your hands until well combined.
4. Divide the mixture into fourths and shape into mini loaves. Place on the prepared baking sheet.
5. In a small bowl, combine the remaining 1 tablespoon tomato paste, the mustard, and water and mix well. Brush over the mini meatloaves.
6. Bake for 18 to 22 minutes or until the meatloaves register 165°F on a meat thermometer.

Nutrition Info:

- Per Serving: Calories: 205 ; Fat : 5 g ;Saturated fat: 1 g ;Sodium: 252 mg

Mustard-roasted Almond Chicken Tenders

Servings: 4
Cooking Time: 15 Minutes
Ingredients:

- ¼ cup low-sodium yellow mustard
- 2 teaspoons yellow mustard seed
- ¼ teaspoon dry mustard
- ⅛ teaspoon garlic powder
- 1 egg white
- 2 tablespoons fresh lemon juice
- ¼ cup almond flour
- ¼ cup ground almonds
- 1 pound chicken tenders

Directions:

1. Preheat the oven to 400°F. Place a wire rack on a baking sheet.
2. In a shallow bowl, combine the yellow mustard, mustard seed, ground mustard, garlic powder, egg white, and lemon juice, and whisk well.
3. To a plate or shallow bowl, add the almond flour and ground almonds, and combine.
4. Dip the chicken tenders into the mustard-egg mixture, then into the almond mixture to coat. Place each tender on the rack on the baking pan as you work.
5. Bake the chicken for 12 to 15 minutes or until a meat thermometer registers 165°F. Serve immediately.

- Per Serving: Calories: 166 ; Fat : 4 g ;Saturated fat: 0 g ;Sodium: 264 mg

Basil Chicken Meatballs

Servings: 20
Cooking Time: 10 Minutes
Ingredients:
- 1 egg white
- ⅓ cup gluten-free (or whole-wheat) bread crumbs
- ½ cup low-sodium chicken broth, divided
- 1 tablespoon fresh lemon juice
- 1 tablespoon freeze-dried chopped chives
- 3 tablespoons minced fresh basil leaves
- ⅛ teaspoon garlic powder
- Pinch salt
- Pinch black pepper
- ¾ pound ground white chicken breast meat

Directions:
1. In a medium bowl, combine the egg white, bread crumbs, 2 tablespoons of the chicken broth, lemon juice, chives, basil, garlic powder, salt, and pepper, and mix well.
2. Add the ground chicken and mix gently but thoroughly until combined.
3. Form into 20 meatballs, about 1 inch in diameter.
4. Heat the remaining 6 tablespoons of the chicken broth in a large nonstick skillet over medium-high heat.
5. Gently add the chicken meatballs in a single layer. Let cook for 5 minutes, then carefully turn and cook another 3 minutes.
6. Lower the heat as the broth reduces, and continue cooking the meatballs, gently shaking the pan occasionally, until the broth has mostly evaporated and the meatballs are browned and cooked to 165°F as tested with a meat thermometer, another 2 to 3 minutes.

Nutrition Info:
- Per Serving: Calories: 130 ; Fat : 3 g ;Saturated fat: 1 g ;Sodium: 162 mg

Crunchy Chicken Coleslaw Salad

Servings: 4
Cooking Time: 7 Minutes
Ingredients:
- 3 (6-ounce) boneless, skinless chicken breasts, cubed
- Pinch salt
- ⅛ teaspoon white pepper
- 1 teaspoon toasted sesame oil
- ¼ cup low-fat mayonnaise
- ¼ cup low-sodium chicken broth
- 2 tablespoons fresh lemon juice
- 1 tablespoon low-sodium yellow mustard
- 2 tablespoons chopped fresh dill
- 4 cups shredded red cabbage
- 1 small yellow summer squash, sliced
- 1 small carrot, shredded
- 2 tablespoons sunflower seeds

Directions:

1. Sprinkle the chicken with the salt and pepper.
2. Heat the sesame oil in a large nonstick skillet. Add the chicken and cook, stirring frequently, until lightly browned and cooked to 165°F when tested with a meat thermometer, about 5 to 7 minutes. Remove from the skillet and set aside.
3. In a large bowl, combine the mayonnaise, chicken broth, lemon juice, mustard, and dill and mix well.
4. Add the cabbage, squash, and carrot to the dressing in the bowl and toss.
5. Add the chicken to the salad and toss.
6. Sprinkle with the sunflower seeds and serve.

Nutrition Info:

- Per Serving: Calories: 256; Fat : 9 g ;Saturated fat: 2 g ;Sodium: 169 mg

Chicken Breasts With Mashed Beans

Servings: 6

Ingredients:

- 3 tablespoons olive oil, divided
- 1 onion, chopped
- 3 cloves garlic, minced
- 1 (14-ounce) can low-sodium cannellini beans
- ½ cup chopped flat-leaf parsley
- ½ teaspoon dried oregano leaves
- 1 teaspoon dried basil leaves
- ¼ cup grated Parmesan cheese
- 3 tablespoons flour
- ¼ teaspoon white pepper
- 6 (4-ounce) boneless, skinless chicken breasts

Directions:

1. In medium saucepan, heat 1 tablespoon olive oil and add onion and garlic. Cook and stir until tender, about 5 minutes. Drain beans, rinse, and drain again.
2. Add to saucepan along with parsley, oregano, and basil. Cook until hot, stirring frequently, about 5 minutes. Using a potato masher, mash the bean mixture. Turn heat to very low.
3. On shallow plate, combine Parmesan, flour, and pepper and mix well. Coat chicken on both sides with cheese mixture. In large skillet, heat remaining 2 tablespoons olive oil over medium heat.
4. Add chicken to skillet; cook for 5 minutes without moving. Carefully turn chicken and cook for 4–6 minutes until thoroughly cooked. Serve with mashed beans.

Nutrition Info:

- Per Serving: Calories:316.30; Fat:10.55 g ;Saturated fat:2.56 g;Sodium: 133.71 mg

Balsamic Blueberry Chicken

Servings: 2
Cooking Time: 25 Min
Ingredients:

- Aluminum foil
- ½ cup fresh blueberries
- 2 tbsp. pine nuts
- ¼ cup cilantro, chopped
- 2 tbsp. balsamic vinegar
- ¼ tsp ground black pepper
- 2 (4 oz) chicken breasts, butterflied

Directions:

1. Heat the olive oil in a medium-sized frying pan over medium Heat the oven to 375°F gas mark 5. Line a baking sheet with aluminum foil.
2. In a medium-sized mixing bowl, add the blueberries, pine nuts, cilantro, balsamic vinegar, and pepper, mix until well combined.
3. Place the chicken breasts on the baking sheet and pour the blueberry mixture on top.
4. Bake for 20 to 25 minutes, until the juices are caramelized, and the inside of the chicken has cooked through. Serve warm.

Nutrition Info:

- Per Serving: Calories: 212 ; Fat: 7 g ;Saturated fat:1 g ;Sodium: 58 mg

Turkey Curry With Fruit

Servings: 6
Ingredients:

- 6 (4-ounce) turkey cutlets
- 1 tablespoon flour
- 1 tablespoon plus
- 1 teaspoon curry powder, divided
- 1 tablespoon olive oil
- 2 pears, chopped
- 1 apple, chopped ½ cup raisins
- 1 tablespoon sugar
- 1/8 teaspoon salt
- 1/3 cup apricot jam

Directions:

1. Preheat oven to 350ºF. Spray a cookie sheet with sides with nonstick cooking spray. Arrange cutlets on prepared cookie sheet. In small bowl, combine flour, 1 tablespoon curry powder, and olive oil and mix well. Spread evenly over cutlets.
2. In medium bowl, combine pears, apple, raisins, sugar, salt, 1 teaspoon curry powder, and apricot jam, and mix well. Divide this mixture over the turkey cutlets.
3. Bake for 35–45 minutes or until turkey is thoroughly cooked and fruit is hot and caramelized. Serve immediately.

Nutrition Info:

- Per Serving: Calories: 371.52; Fat: 11.15 g ;Saturated fat: 2.80 g ;Sodium: 121.35 mg

Cashew Chicken

Servings: 2
Cooking Time: 5 Min
Ingredients:
- 2 tsp olive oil
  - 2 tsp garlic, minced, divided
  - ½ cup red onion, chopped
  - 8 oz ground chicken
  - 1 tsp ginger, grated
  - 3 tbsp. unsalted cashew butter
  - 4 tbsp. water
  - 6 large green leaf lettuce leaves
  - ½ cup unsalted cashew nuts, roughly chopped

Directions:
1. Heat the olive oil in a medium-sized frying pan over medium heat. Add the 1 tsp garlic and onion, cook for 1 to 2 minutes, until translucent.
2. Add the chicken and separate using a fork. Continue mixing for 5 minutes until lightly golden and cooked through.
3. In a small-sized mixing bowl, add the ginger, remaining 1 tsp garlic, cashew butter, and water, mix to combine.
4. Add the cashew mixture to the ground chicken. Cook for 1 minute until all flavors have combined.
5. Divide the cashew chicken mixture into the lettuce cups and serve topped with the cashew nuts.

Nutrition Info:
- Per Serving: Calories: 414 ; Fat: 21 g ;Saturated fat: 4 g ;Sodium: 211 mg

Nutty Coconut Chicken With Fruit Sauce

Servings: 4
Cooking Time: 15 Minutes
Ingredients:
- ¼ cup ground almonds
- ⅓ cup unsweetened flaked coconut
- ¼ cup coconut flour
- Pinch salt
- ⅛ teaspoon white pepper
- 1 egg white
- 1 (16-ounce) package chicken tenders
- 1 cup sliced strawberries
- 1 cup raspberries
- ⅓ cup unsweetened white grape juice
- 1 tablespoon lemon juice
- ½ teaspoon dried thyme leaves
- ⅓ cup dried cherries

Directions:
1. Preheat the oven to 400°F. Place a wire rack on a baking sheet.
2. In a shallow plate, combine the ground almonds, flaked coconut, coconut flour, salt, and white pepper, and mix well.
3. In a shallow bowl, beat the egg white just until foamy.
4. Dip the chicken tenders into the egg white, then into the almond mixture to coat. Place on the wire rack as you work.
5. Bake the chicken tenders for 14 to 16 minutes or until the chicken is cooked to 165°F when tested with a meat thermometer.
6. While the chicken is baking, in a food processor or blender, combine the strawberries, raspberries, grape juice, lemon juice, and thyme leaves and process or blend until smooth.

7. Pour the mixture into a small saucepan, and add the dried cherries. Bring to a simmer over medium heat. Simmer for 3 minutes, then remove the pan from the heat and set aside.
8. Serve the chicken with the warm fruit sauce.

Nutrition Info:
- Per Serving: Calories: 281 ; Fat : 8 g ;Saturated fat: 3 g ;Sodium: 124 mg

Tandoori Turkey Pizzas

Servings: 4
Cooking Time: 18 Minutes
Ingredients:
- 4 (6½-inch) whole-wheat pita breads
- 1 teaspoon olive oil
- 1 onion, chopped
- 4 cloves garlic, minced
- ½ pound ground turkey
- 1 (8-ounce) can no-salt-added tomato sauce
- 2 teaspoons curry powder
- ½ teaspoon smoked paprika
- ¼ teaspoon ground cumin
- ⅛ teaspoon cayenne pepper
- ¼ cup crumbled feta cheese
- 3 tablespoons low-fat plain Greek yogurt

Directions:
1. Preheat the oven to 425°F. Place the pita breads on a baking sheet lined with aluminum foil and set aside.
2. In a large skillet, heat the olive oil over medium heat. Add the onion and garlic and cook, stirring frequently, for 2 minutes.
3. Add the ground turkey and sauté, breaking up the meat. Cook for 5 minutes or until the turkey is no longer pink.
4. Add the tomato sauce, curry powder, paprika, cumin, and cayenne pepper to the sauce and bring to a simmer. Simmer over low heat for 1 minute.
5. Top the pita "pizzas" evenly with the turkey mixture. Sprinkle each with the feta cheese.
6. Bake for 10 to 12 minutes or until the pizzas are hot. Drizzle each pizza with the yogurt and serve immediately.

Nutrition Info:
- Per Serving: Calories: 308 ; Fat : 6 g ;Saturated fat: 2 g ;Sodium: 779 mg

Chicken Breasts With Salsa

Servings: 4
Ingredients:
- 2 tablespoons lime juice, divided
- 1 egg white
- 1 cup whole-grain cereal, crushed
- 1 teaspoon dried thyme leaves
- ¼ teaspoon pepper
- 4 (4-ounce) boneless, skinless chicken breasts
- 1 cup Super Spicy Salsa
- 1 jalapeño pepper, minced

Directions:
1. Preheat oven to 375ºF. Line a cookie sheet with a wire rack and set aside. In small bowl, combine 1 tablespoon lime juice and egg white; beat until frothy. On shallow plate, combine crushed cereal, thyme, and pepper.

2. Dip chicken into egg white mixture, then into cereal mixture to coat. Place on prepared cookie sheet. Bake for 20–25 minutes or until chicken is thoroughly cooked and coating is crisp.
3. Meanwhile, in small saucepan combine remaining 1 tablespoon lime juice, salsa, and jalapeño pepper. Heat through, stirring occasionally. Serve with chicken.

Nutrition Info:
• Per Serving: Calories: 264.05; Fat: 4.43 g ;Saturated fat:1.18 g ;Sodium: 146.85 mg

Sautéed Chicken With Roasted Garlic Sauce

Servings: 4
Ingredients:
• 1 head Roasted Garlic
• 1/3 cup Low-Sodium Chicken Broth
• ½ teaspoon dried oregano leaves
• 4 (4-ounce) boneless, skinless chicken breasts
• ¼ cup flour
• 1/8 teaspoon salt
• 1/8 teaspoon pepper
• ¼ teaspoon paprika
• 2 tablespoons olive oil

Directions:
1. Squeeze garlic cloves from the skins and combine in small saucepan with chicken broth and oregano leaves.
   1. On shallow plate, combine flour, salt, pepper, and paprika. Dip chicken into this mixture to coat.
   2. In large skillet, heat 2 tablespoons olive oil. At the same time, place the saucepan with the garlic mixture over medium heat. Add the chicken to the hot olive oil; cook for 5 minutes without moving. Then carefully turn chicken and cook for 4–7 minutes longer until chicken is thoroughly cooked.
   3. Stir garlic sauce with wire whisk until blended. Serve with the chicken.

Nutrition Info:
• Per Serving: Calories: 267.01; Fat: 7.78g ;Saturated fat:1.65 g ;Sodium: 158.61 mg

Pork And Beef Mains Recipes

Pork And Beef Mains Recipes

Spinach And Kale Salad With Spicy Pork

Servings: 4
Cooking Time: 10 Minutes
Ingredients:

- 1 tablespoon olive oil, divided
- 2 tablespoons buttermilk
- 2 tablespoons lime juice
- 2 tablespoons low-sodium yellow mustard
- ½ teaspoon fennel seed
- 1 pound plain pork tenderloin
- Pinch salt
- ⅛ teaspoon cayenne pepper
- 2 teaspoons chili powder
- 3 cups baby spinach leaves, rinsed and dried
- 2 cups torn kale leaves, rinsed and dried, stem removed
- 1 carrot, shredded
- 1 red bell pepper, seeded and chopped
- 1 tablespoon crumbled soft goat cheese

Directions:

1. In a small bowl, make the dressing: Combine 2 teaspoons of the olive oil, the buttermilk, lime juice, mustard, and fennel seed, and mix well with a whisk until combined. Set aside.
2. Slice the pork tenderloin into 1-inch pieces and put into a medium bowl. Sprinkle with the salt, cayenne pepper, and chili powder.
3. Heat the remaining 1 teaspoon olive oil in a large nonstick skillet. Add the tenderloin pieces, cut side down. Cook for 4 minutes without turning.
4. Turn the pork and cook for 2 to 3 minutes or until the pork registers 150°F on a meat thermometer. Remove from the pan to a clean plate and cover with an aluminum foil tent to keep warm.
5. In a large salad bowl, toss the spinach, kale, carrot, and bell pepper. Add the salad dressing and toss to coat. Top with the pork and goat cheese, and serve immediately.

Nutrition Info:

- Per Serving: Calories: 207 ; Fat: 9 g ;Saturated fat: 2 g ;Sodium: 213 mg

Beef Rollups With Pesto

Servings: 6

Ingredients:

- ½ cup packed basil leaves
- ½ cup packed baby spinach leaves
- 3 cloves garlic, minced
- 1/3 cup toasted chopped hazelnuts
- 1/8 teaspoon white pepper
- 2 tablespoons grated Parmesan cheese
- 2 tablespoons olive oil
- 2 tablespoons water
- 3 tablespoons flour
- ½ teaspoon paprika
- 6 (4-ounce) top round steaks, ¼″ thick
- 2 oil-packed sun-dried tomatoes, minced
- 1 tablespoon canola oil
- 1 cup Low-Sodium Beef Broth

Directions:

1. In blender or food processor, combine basil, spinach, garlic, hazelnuts, and white pepper, and blend or process until finely chopped. Add Parmesan and blend again. Add olive oil and blend until a paste forms, then add water and blend.
2. On shallow plate, combine flour, and paprika and mix well. Place beef between sheets of waxed paper and pound until A" thick. Spread pesto on one side of the pounded beef and sprinkle with tomatoes. Roll up, fastening closed with tooth-picks.
3. Dredge rollups in flour mixture. Heat canola oil in large saucepan and brown rollups on all sides, about 5 minutes total. Pour beef broth into pan and bring to a simmer. Cover, reduce heat to low, and simmer for 40–50 minutes or until beef is tender.

Nutrition Info:

- Per Serving: Calories: 290.23 ; Fat:18.73g ;Saturated fat:3.90 g ;Sodium:95.79 mg

Pork Quesadillas

Servings: 6

Ingredients:

- 1/3 cup low-fat sour cream
- 1 cup shredded part-skim mozzarella cheese
- 1 cup chopped Mustard Pork Tenderloin (below)
- 1 avocado, chopped
- 1 jalapeño pepper, minced
- 10 (6-inch) corn tortillas
- 2 tablespoons olive oil

Directions:

1. In medium bowl, combine sour cream, cheese, pork tenderloin, avocado, and jalapeño pepper and mix gently.
2. Divide mixture among half the tortillas, placing the remaining half of tortillas on top to make sandwiches. Heat griddle and brush with olive oil. Place quesadillas on the griddle; cover and grill for 2–3 minutes on each side until tortillas are crisp and cheese is melted. Cut into quarters and serve.

Nutrition Info:

- Per Serving: Calories: 315.36 ; Fat:16.67 g ;Saturated fat:5.55 g ;Sodium:161.17 mg

Classic Spaghetti And Meatballs

Servings: X
Cooking Time: 20 Minutes
Ingredients:

- Nonstick olive oil cooking spray
- 6 ounces extra-lean ground beef
- 1 large egg white
- ¼ cup ground almonds
- 2 teaspoons chopped fresh parsley
- ¼ teaspoon garlic powder
- Pinch sea salt
- Pinch freshly ground black pepper
- 2 cups Double Tomato Sauce or your favorite low-sodium marinara sauce
- 4 ounces dry spaghetti

Directions:

1. Preheat the oven to 400°F.
2. Line a baking sheet with parchment paper and spray it lightly with cooking spray. Set aside.
3. In a medium bowl, combine the ground beef, egg white, almonds, parsley, garlic powder, salt, and pepper until well mixed. Form the meat mixture into 12 meatballs and spread out on the baking sheet.
4. Bake the meatballs until cooked through, about 20 minutes. Remove from the oven and set aside.
5. While the meatballs are cooking, warm the sauce in a medium saucepan over medium heat. Cook the spaghetti according to package instructions.
6. Drain the pasta and serve topped with sauce and meatballs.

Nutrition Info:

- Per Serving: Calories: 574 ; Fat: 12 g ;Saturated fat: 2 g ;Sodium: 443 mg

Cowboy Steak With Chimichurri Sauce

Servings: 4–6
Ingredients:

- 1 cup chopped parsley
- ¼ cup minced fresh oregano leaves
- ¼ cup extra-virgin olive oil
- 2 tablespoons lemon juice
- 3 tablespoons sherry vinegar
- 6 cloves garlic, minced
- 1/8 teaspoon salt
- ¼ teaspoon pepper
- 1 pound flank steak
- 2 tablespoons red wine
- 2 tablespoons olive oil

Directions:

1. In blender or food processor, combine parsley, oregano, olive oil, lemon juice, sherry vinegar, garlic, salt, and pepper; blend or process until smooth. Pour into small bowl, cover, and refrigerate until ready to use.
2. Pierce flank steak all over with a fork. Place in large heavy-duty zip-close freezer bag and add red wine and olive oil. Seal bag and squish to mix. Place in pan and refrigerate for 8–12 hours.
3. When ready to eat, prepare and preheat grill. Grill steak for 6–10 minutes, turning once, until desired doneness. Remove from grill and let stand, covered, for 10 minutes. Slice thinly against the grain and serve with the Chimichurri Sauce.

Nutrition Info:
- Per Serving: Calories:244.50; Fat:18.59 g ;Saturated fat: 5.20 g ;Sodium: 117.31 mg

Pork Scallops Françoise

Servings: 4
Ingredients:
- 3 tablespoons flour
- 1/8 teaspoon salt
- 1/8 teaspoon pepper
- 1 egg white, slightly beaten
- 4 (3-ounce) pork scallops
- 1 tablespoon olive oil
- 1 tablespoon butter
- 3 cloves garlic, minced
- 2 tablespoons lemon juice
- 2 tablespoons chopped fresh parsley

Directions:
1. On plate, combine flour, salt, and pepper. Place egg white in shallow bowl. If necessary, pound scallops until they are A" thick. Dip scallops into flour, then into egg whites.
2. Heat olive oil and butter in nonstick skillet. Add garlic; cook for 1 minute. Then add coated pork; brown for 2–3 minutes per side. Add lemon juice; cook for 2–3 minutes or until pork is cooked and tender. Sprinkle with parsley and serve immediately.

Nutrition Info:
- Per Serving: Calories: 224.74; Fat:11.25 mg ;Saturated fat:4.04 mg ;Sodium: 158.05 mg

Beef And Avocado Quesadillas

Servings: 4
Cooking Time: 10 Minutes
Ingredients:
- ½ pound 98% lean ground beef
- 1 small onion, chopped
- 3 cloves garlic, minced
- 8 medium mushrooms, sliced
- 1 cup shredded carrot
- ½ cup low-sodium salsa
- ½ cup low-fat mozzarella cheese
- ½ avocado, peeled and diced
- 4 whole-wheat flour tortillas

Directions:
1. In a large nonstick skillet, sauté the ground beef, onion, garlic, mushrooms, and carrot, stirring to break up the meat, until the meat is browned and fully cooked, about 5 to 6 minutes. Drain if necessary.
2. Transfer the beef mixture to a medium bowl and stir in the salsa.
3. Place the tortillas on the work surface. Divide the meat mixture among them, placing the meat on half of the tortilla. Top with the cheese and avocado. Fold the tortillas over and press gently into a quesadilla.
4. Rinse and dry the nonstick skillet.
5. One at a time, place the quesadillas into the skillet over medium heat, and cook for 2 to 3 minutes on each side. Cut the quesadillas in half and serve immediately.

Nutrition Info:
- Per Serving: Calories: 237 ; Fat: 9 g ;Saturated fat: 3 g ;Sodium: 344 mg

Chops With Mint And Garlic

Servings: 4

Ingredients:

- 3 tablespoons minced fresh mint
- 1 tablespoon minced garlic
- 2 tablespoons olive oil
- 1 tablespoon lemon juice
- 4 (4-ounce) pork chops
- 1/8 teaspoon salt
- 1/8 teaspoon white pepper

Directions:

1. Prepare and preheat grill. In small bowl, combine mint, garlic, olive oil, and lemon juice and mix well.
2. Sprinkle pork chops with salt and pepper. Brush with sauce and place on grill. Grill 6″ from medium coals for 5–6 minutes per side until internal temperatures reach 155ºF, brushing with mint sauce. Discard any remaining mint sauce. Let chops stand for 5 minutes, then serve.

Nutrition Info:

- Per Serving: Calories:251.09 ; Fat:17.56 g ;Saturated fat:4.97 g ;Sodium: 242.71 mg

Pork Goulash

Servings: 4

Cooking Time: 15 Minutes

Ingredients:

- ½ pound lean ground pork
- 2 onions, chopped
- 8 ounces sliced button mushrooms
- 4 cloves garlic, minced
- 3 stalks celery, sliced
- ½ cup grated carrot
- 2 teaspoons smoked paprika
- Pinch salt
- ⅛ teaspoon white pepper
- 1 (14-ounce) can no-salt-added diced tomatoes
- 1 (8-ounce) can no-salt-added tomato sauce
- 2 tablespoons tomato paste
- ½ cup water
- 1 cup whole-wheat orzo

Directions:

1. In a large skillet over medium-high, sauté the pork, onions, mushrooms, garlic, celery, and carrot for 4 minutes, stirring to break up the pork, until the meat is almost cooked through.
2. Add the paprika, salt, white pepper, tomatoes, tomato sauce, tomato paste, and water, and bring to a simmer. Simmer for 1 minute.
3. Add the orzo to the skillet and stir, making sure that the pasta is covered by liquid. Simmer for 10 to 12 minutes or until the pasta is cooked al dente. Serve immediately.

Nutrition Info:

- Per Serving: Calories:299 ; Fat:7 g ;Saturated fat: 2 g ;Sodium: 128 mg

Beef Burrito Skillet

Servings: 4
Cooking Time: 15 Minutes
Ingredients:

- ¾ pound extra-lean ground beef
- 1 onion, chopped
- 4 cloves garlic, minced
- 1 jalapeño pepper, seeded and minced
- 1 tablespoon chili powder
- ½ teaspoon cumin
- 1 (16-ounce) can no-salt-added pinto beans, rinsed and drained
- 1 tomato, chopped
- 1 cup frozen corn, thawed
- ½ cup low-sodium salsa
- 3 corn tortillas, cut into 1-inch strips
- 2 tablespoons crumbled cotija cheese
- ¼ cup low-fat sour cream

Directions:

1. In a large skillet, sauté the ground beef, onion, garlic, and jalapeño pepper, stirring to break up the meat, until the beef is browned, about 5 to 7 minutes.
2. Add the chili powder and cumin, and stir.
3. Add in the pinto beans, tomato, corn, and salsa, and bring to a simmer. Simmer for 5 minutes, stirring occasionally.
4. Stir in the corn tortillas and cook for 3 to 4 minutes. Top with the cheese and sour cream, and serve.

Nutrition Info:

- Per Serving: Calories: 403 ; Fat: 10 g ;Saturated fat: 4 g ;Sodium: 215 mg

Pork Scallops With Spinach

Servings: 6
Ingredients:

- 3 tablespoons flour
- 1/8 teaspoon salt
- 1/8 teaspoon pepper
- 6 (3-ounce) pork scallops
- 2 tablespoons olive oil
- 1 onion, chopped
- 1 (10-ounce) package frozen chopped spinach, thawed
- 1 tablespoon flour
- ½ teaspoon celery seed
- 1/3 cup nonfat light cream
- 1/3 cup part-skim ricotta cheese
- ½ cup dried breadcrumbs, divided
- 2 tablespoons grated Romano cheese

Directions:

1. Preheat oven to 350ºF. On plate, combine 3 tablespoons flour, salt, and pepper and mix well. Pound pork scallops, if necessary, to A1/8" thickness.
2. Heat olive oil in nonstick pan over medium-high heat. Dredge pork in flour mixture and sauté in pan, turning once, until just browned, about 1 minute per side. Remove to a baking dish.
3. Add onion to pan; cook and stir for 3 minutes. Drain spinach well and add to pan; cook and stir until liquid evaporates. Add flour and celery seed; cook and stir for 1 minute.

4. Stir in light cream; cook and stir until thickened, about 3 minutes. Remove from heat and add ricotta cheese and half of the breadcrumbs.
5. Divide spinach mixture on top of pork in baking dish. Top with remaining breadcrumbs and Romano. Bake for 10–15 minutes or until pork is tender and thoroughly cooked. Serve immediately.

Nutrition Info:
- Per Serving: Calories: 298.66; Fat: 12.60 g ;Saturated fat:4.08 g ;Sodium: 303.25 mg

Sirloin Meatballs In Sauce

Servings: 6
Ingredients:
- 1 tablespoon olive oil
- 3 cloves garlic, minced
- ½ cup minced onion
- 2 egg whites
- ½ cup dry breadcrumbs
- ¼ cup grated Parmesan cheese
- ½ teaspoon crushed fennel seeds
- ½ teaspoon dried oregano leaves
- 2 teaspoons Worcestershire sauce
- 1/8 teaspoon pepper
- 1/8 teaspoon crushed red pepper flakes
- 1 pound 95% lean ground sirloin
- 1 recipe Spaghetti Sauce

Directions:
1. In small saucepan, heat olive oil over medium heat. Add garlic and onion; cook and stir until tender, about 5 minutes. Remove from heat and place in large mixing bowl.
2. Add egg whites, breadcrumbs, Parmesan, fennel, oregano, Worcestershire sauce, pepper, and pepper flakes and mix well. Add sirloin; mix gently but thoroughly until combined. Form into 12 meatballs.
3. In large nonstick saucepan, place Spaghetti Sauce and bring to a simmer. Carefully add meatballs to sauce. Return to a simmer, partially cover, and simmer for 15–25 minutes or until meatballs are thoroughly cooked.

Nutrition Info:
- Per Serving: Calories: 367.93; Fat: 13.56 g ;Saturated fat: 3.91 g;Sodium: 305.47 mg

Lemon Basil Pork Medallions

Servings: 4
Cooking Time: 15 Minutes
Ingredients:
- 1 pound plain pork tenderloin
- ½ teaspoon dried basil leaves
- Pinch salt
- ⅛ teaspoon lemon pepper
- 3 tablespoons cornstarch
- 1 teaspoon olive oil
- 3 cloves garlic, minced
- 1 cup chicken broth
- 3 tablespoons fresh lemon juice
- 1 teaspoon fresh lemon zest
- 3 tablespoons chopped fresh basil

Directions:

1. Slice the pork tenderloin crosswise into 1-inch slices.
2. Place the slices on a piece of plastic wrap or parchment paper. Cover with another piece of plastic wrap. Put on a cutting board.
3. Using a rolling pin or meat mallet, gently pound the slices until they are about ½-inch thick.
4. On a plate, combine the dried basil, salt, lemon pepper, and cornstarch. Add the tenderloin slices and toss to coat.
5. Heat a large nonstick skillet over medium heat and add the olive oil.
6. Add half the tenderloin slices and cook until browned, about 2 minutes (it's important to not crowd the pan). Turn the pork and cook 1 to 2 minutes on the other side. Remove from the skillet to a clean plate. Repeat with remaining pork.
7. Add the garlic to the pan and cook, stirring constantly, for 1 minute. Add the chicken broth, lemon juice, and lemon zest, and bring to a simmer.
8. Put the pork slices back in the skillet, and simmer for 2 to 3 minutes until sauce thickens slightly and is cooked to 145°F on a meat thermometer. Stir in the fresh basil leaves, and serve.

Nutrition Info:
- Per Serving: Calories: 170 ; Fat: 6 g ;Saturated fat: 2 g ;Sodium: 328 mg

Maple-balsamic Pork Chops

Servings: X
Cooking Time: 20 Minutes
Ingredients:
- ¼ cup low-sodium chicken broth
- 2 tablespoons maple syrup
- 1 tablespoon balsamic vinegar
- ¼ teaspoon chopped fresh thyme
- 2 (4-ounce) boneless pork top-loin chops
- Sea salt
- Freshly ground black pepper
- Nonstick olive oil cooking spray

Directions:

1. In a small bowl, stir together the chicken broth, maple syrup, vinegar, and thyme.
2. Season the pork chops on both sides with sea salt and pepper.
3. Place a medium skillet over medium-high heat and spray generously with cooking spray. Add the pork chops and cook, about 6 minutes on each side.
4. Add the sauce to the skillet and turn the chops to coat completely.
5. Continue to cook until the pork chops are cooked through, about 6 minutes more, turning once.
6. Let the pork rest for 10 minutes and serve.

Nutrition Info:
- Per Serving: Calories:163 ; Fat: 7 g ;Saturated fat: 2 g ;Sodium: 212 mg

Sliced Flank Steak With Sherry-mustard Sauce

Servings: X
Cooking Time: 30 Minutes
Ingredients:

- 1 (6-ounce) flank steak, fat trimmed
- Sea salt
- Freshly ground black pepper
- Nonstick olive oil cooking spray
- 1 teaspoon canola oil
- 2 shallots, chopped
- ½ cup sherry
- 1 cup low-sodium beef broth
- 2 teaspoons Dijon mustard
- ½ teaspoon chopped fresh thyme

Directions:

1. Lightly season the steak with salt and pepper.
2. Generously coat a medium skillet with cooking spray and let it preheat over high heat on the stove. Sear the steak until browned and cooked to your desired doneness, 6 minutes per side for medium. Set the steak aside to rest.
3. While the steak is resting, warm the canola oil in the skillet. Add the shallots and sauté until softened, about 3 minutes.
4. Add the sherry to the skillet and bring to a boil. Cook until the liquid is reduced by half, about 4 minutes. Stir in the broth, mustard, and thyme and continue boiling until the sauce is reduced to about ½ cup, about 5 minutes.
5. Slice the steak thinly across the grain and serve with the sauce.

Nutrition Info:

- Per Serving: Calories: 268 ; Fat: 13 g ;Saturated fat: 5 g ;Sodium: 278 mg

Cabbage Roll Sauté

Servings: X
Cooking Time: 30 Minutes
Ingredients:

- 4 cups water
- ½ cup brown rice, rinsed
- Nonstick olive oil cooking spray
- 6 ounces extra-lean ground beef
- ¼ small sweet onion, chopped
- ½ teaspoon minced garlic
- 2 cups crushed tomatoes
- 1 tablespoon brown sugar
- 2 teaspoons balsamic vinegar
- ¼ teaspoon paprika
- 2 cups thinly shredded cabbage
- 2 teaspoons chopped fresh parsley, for garnish

Directions:

1. Warm the water in a medium saucepan over high heat and bring to a boil.
2. Add the rice and reduce the heat to medium-low. Simmer until the rice is tender, about 30 minutes.
3. Drain any excess water and set the rice aside, covered, to keep warm.
4. Generously coat a large skillet with cooking spray and place over medium-high heat.
5. Add the beef and cook until browned, breaking it up, 5 to 7 minutes.
6. Stir in the onion and garlic and sauté until the vegetables are softened, about 3 minutes.

7. Stir in the crushed tomatoes, sugar, vinegar, and paprika and bring the sauce to a boil.
8. Stir in the cabbage and reduce the heat to low. Simmer until the cabbage is very tender, 10 to 12 minutes.
9. Serve the cabbage roll mixture over the rice, topped with parsley.

Nutrition Info:
- Per Serving: Calories: 473 ; Fat: 9 g ;Saturated fat: 3 g ;Sodium: 328 mg

Mustard And Thyme–crusted Beef Tenderloin

Servings: X
Cooking Time: 15 Minutes
Ingredients:
- ¼ cup grainy mustard
- 1 tablespoon chopped fresh thyme
- 1 teaspoon chopped fresh parsley
- 2 (3-ounce) beef tenderloin steaks, fat trimmed
- Sea salt
- Freshly ground black pepper
- Nonstick olive oil cooking spray

Directions:
1. Preheat the oven for 400°F.
2. In a small bowl, stir together the mustard, thyme, and parsley until well blended.
3. Lightly season the beef with salt and pepper.
4. Coat a medium oven-safe skillet with cooking spray and place over medium-high heat.
5. Add the beef and cook until browned on both sides, about 4 minutes per side.
6. Remove the skillet from the heat and spread the mustard mixture all over each steak.
7. Place the skillet in the oven and roast the beef until desired doneness, about 8 minutes for medium.
8. Let the meat rest for 10 minutes and serve.

Nutrition Info:
- Per Serving: Calories: 224 ; Fat: 11 g ;Saturated fat: 5 g ;Sodium: 206 mg

Pork Chops With Cabbage

Servings: 6
Ingredients:
- 1 red onion, chopped
- 4 cloves garlic, minced
- 3 cups chopped red cabbage
- 3 cups chopped green cabbage
- 1 apple, chopped
- 6 (3-ounce) boneless pork chops
- 1/8 teaspoon white pepper
- 1 tablespoon olive oil
- ¼ cup brown sugar
- ¼ cup apple cider vinegar
- 1 tablespoon mustard

Directions:
1. In 4- to 5-quart slow cooker, combine onion, garlic, cabbages, and apple and mix well.
2. Trim pork chops of any excess fat and sprinkle with pepper. Heat olive oil in large saucepan over medium heat. Brown chops on just one side, about 3 minutes. Add to slow cooker with vegetables.

3. In small bowl, combine brown sugar, vinegar, and mustard and mix well. Pour into slow cooker. Cover and cook on low for 7–8 hours or until pork and cabbage are tender. Serve immediately.

Nutrition Info:
- Per Serving: Calories: 242.86 ; Fat: 10.57 g ;Saturated fat:3.37 g ;Sodium:364.80 mg

Corned-beef Hash

Servings: 6
Ingredients:
- 2 tablespoons olive oil
- 2 onions, chopped
- 4 cloves garlic, minced
- 8 fingerling potatoes, chopped
- 4 carrots, chopped
- ¼ cup water
- ½ pound deli corned beef, diced
- 1/8 teaspoon ground cloves
- 1/8 teaspoon white pepper
- 3 tablespoons low-sodium chili sauce

Directions:
1. Place olive oil in large saucepan; heat over medium heat. Add onion and garlic; cook and stir for 3 minutes. Add potatoes and carrots; cook and stir until potatoes are partially cooked, about 5 minutes.
2. Add water, corned beef, cloves, pepper, and chili sauce. Stir well, then cover, reduce heat to low, and simmer for 10–15 minutes or until blended and potatoes are cooked. Serve immediately.

Nutrition Info:
- Per Serving: Calories: 283.21 ; Fat:11.97 g ;Saturated fat: 3.09 g;Sodium:472.63 mg

Fiery Pork Stir-fry

Servings: X
Cooking Time: 20 Minutes
Ingredients:
* For the sauce
* ¼ cup low-sodium chicken broth
* 1 tablespoon low-sodium tamari sauce
* 1 tablespoon honey
* 1 teaspoon cornstarch
* 1 teaspoon rice vinegar
* 1 teaspoon peeled, grated ginger
* ½ teaspoon minced garlic
* ⅛ teaspoon red pepper flakes
* For the stir-fry
* 2 teaspoons sesame oil
* 1 (8-ounce) pork tenderloin, cut into ¼-inch slices
* 1 carrot, thinly sliced
* 1 red bell pepper, thinly sliced
* 1 cup sliced mushrooms
* 1 cup small broccoli florets
* 1 cup green beans, cut into 1-inch pieces
* 1 scallion, green part only, thinly sliced, for garnish
* 2 tablespoons chopped cashews, for garnish

Directions:
1. To make the sauce
2. In a small bowl, stir together the chicken broth, tamari, honey, cornstarch, vinegar, ginger, garlic, and red pepper flakes.
3. Set aside.
4. To make the stir-fry
5. In a large skillet, warm the sesame oil over medium-high heat.
6. Add the pork and sauté until it is just cooked through, about 12 minutes.
7. Stir in the carrots, bell pepper, and mushrooms and stir-fry until the vegetables are tender, about 5 minutes.
8. Stir in the broccoli and green beans and stir-fry until the veggies are tender, about 4 minutes.
9. Add the sauce to the skillet and cook until the sauce thickens, about 3 minutes.
10. Stir to coat and serve topped with the scallions and cashews.

Nutrition Info:
* Per Serving: Calories: 321 ; Fat: 11 g ;Saturated fat: 2 g ;Sodium: 356 mg

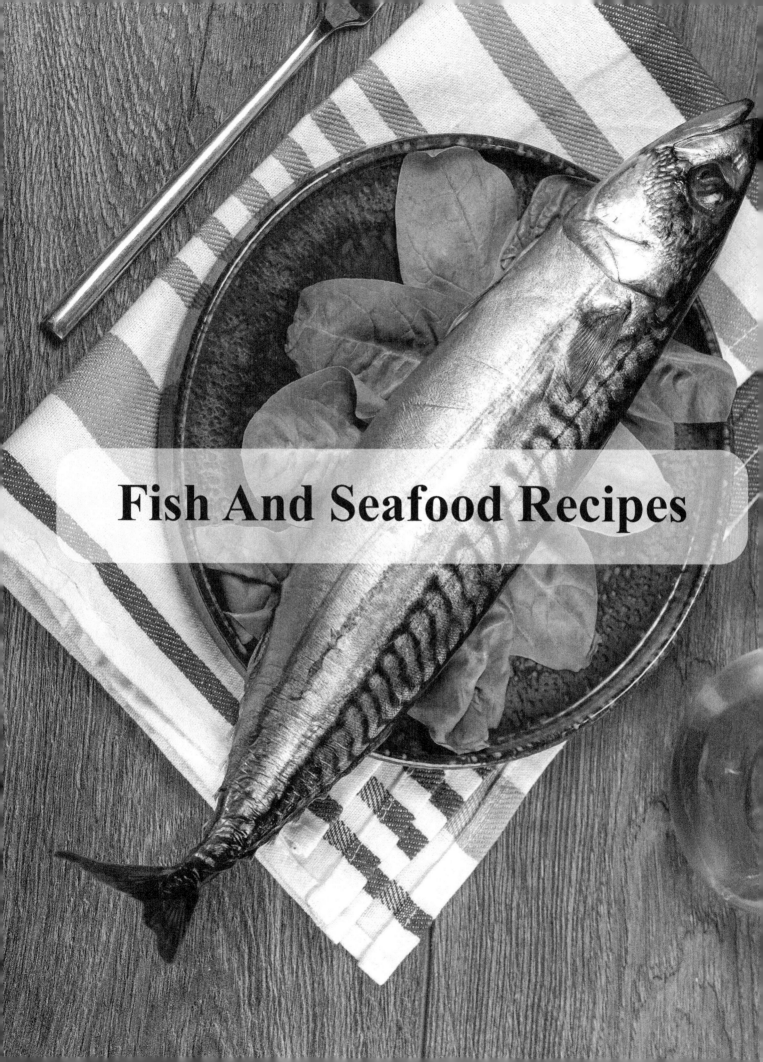

Fish And Seafood Recipes

Fish And Seafood Recipes

Grilled Scallops With Gremolata

Servings: 4
Cooking Time: 6 Minutes
Ingredients:

- 2 scallions, cut into pieces
- ¾ cup packed fresh flat-leaf parsley
- ¼ cup packed fresh basil leaves
- 1 teaspoon lemon zest
- 3 tablespoons fresh lemon juice
- 1 tablespoon olive oil
- 20 sea scallops
- 2 teaspoons butter, melted
- Pinch salt
- ⅛ teaspoon lemon pepper

Directions:

1. Prepare and preheat the grill to medium-high. Make sure the grill rack is clean.
2. Meanwhile, make the gremolata. In a blender or food processor, combine the scallions, parsley, basil, lemon zest, lemon juice, and olive oil. Blend or process until the herbs are finely chopped. Pour into a small bowl and set aside.
3. Put the scallops on a plate. If the scallops have a small tough muscle attached to them, remove and discard it. Brush the melted butter over the scallops. Sprinkle with the salt and the lemon pepper.
4. Place the scallops in a grill basket, if you have one. If not, place a sheet of heavy-duty foil on the grill, punch some holes in it, and arrange the scallops evenly across it.
5. Grill the scallops for 2 to 3 minutes per side, turning once, until opaque. Drizzle with the gremolata and serve.

Nutrition Info:

- Per Serving: Calories: 190 ; Fat: 7 g ;Saturated fat: 2 g;Sodium: 336 mg

Halibut Parcels

Servings: 4
Cooking Time: 15 Min
Ingredients:

- Aluminum foil
- 4 cups kale, stems removed and shredded
- 2 cups button mushrooms, sliced
- 4 (4 oz) halibut fillets
- ½ tsp seafood seasoning
- ½ tsp fine sea salt
- ¼ tsp ground black pepper
- ¼ cup spring onion, chopped
- 2 tbsp. olive oil

Directions:

1. Heat the oven to 425°F gas mark 7.
2. Prepare the aluminum foil by tearing them into squares, big enough for the fillets and vegetables.

3. Place 1 cup of kale and ½ cup of mushroom onto each foil square.
4. Place the halibut fillet on top of each parcel. Season with seafood seasoning, salt and pepper.
5. Sprinkle the spring onion over this and drizzle with olive oil.
6. Fold the foil to seal in the halibut and vegetables.
7. Place on a baking sheet and bake for 15 minutes. Remove from the oven and carefully unfold the parcels.

Nutrition Info:
- Per Serving: Calories:155 ; Fat: 7 g ;Saturated fat: 1 g ;Sodium: 435 mg

Cod Satay

Servings: 4
Cooking Time: 15 Minutes
Ingredients:
- 2 teaspoons olive oil, divided
- 1 small onion, diced
- 2 cloves garlic, minced
- ⅓ cup low-fat coconut milk
- 1 tomato, chopped
- 2 tablespoons low-fat peanut butter
- 1 tablespoon packed brown sugar
- ⅓ cup low-sodium vegetable broth
- 2 teaspoons low-sodium soy sauce
- ⅛ teaspoon ground ginger
- Pinch red pepper flakes
- 4 (6-ounce) cod fillets
- ⅛ teaspoon white pepper

Directions:
1. In a small saucepan, heat 1 teaspoon of the olive oil over medium heat.
2. Add the onion and garlic, and cook, stirring frequently for 3 minutes.
3. Add the coconut milk, tomato, peanut butter, brown sugar, broth, soy sauce, ginger, and red pepper flakes, and bring to a simmer, stirring with a whisk until the sauce combines. Simmer for 2 minutes, then remove the satay sauce from the heat and set aside.
4. Season the cod with the white pepper.
5. Heat a large nonstick skillet with the remaining 1 teaspoon olive oil, and add the cod fillets. Cook for 3 minutes, then turn and cook for 3 to 4 minutes more or until the fish flakes when tested with a fork.
6. Cover the fish with the satay sauce and serve immediately.

Nutrition Info:
- Per Serving: Calories: 255 ; Fat: 10 g ;Saturated fat: 5 g;Sodium: 222 mg

Salmon With Farro Pilaf

Servings: 4
Cooking Time: 25 Minutes
Ingredients:
- ½ cup farro
- 1¼ cups low-sodium vegetable broth
- 4 (4-ounce) salmon fillets
- Pinch salt
- ½ teaspoon dried marjoram leaves
- ⅛ teaspoon white pepper
- ¼ cup dried cherries
- ¼ cup dried currants
- 1 cup fresh baby spinach leaves
- 1 tablespoon orange juice

Directions:
1. Preheat the oven to 400°F. Line a baking sheet with parchment paper and set aside.
2. In a medium saucepan over medium heat, combine the farro and the vegetable broth and bring to a simmer. Reduce the heat to low and simmer, partially covered, for 25 minutes, or until the farro is tender.
3. Meanwhile, sprinkle the salmon with the salt, marjoram, and white pepper and place on the prepared baking sheet.
4. When the farro has cooked for 10 minutes, bake the salmon in the oven for 12 to 15 minutes, or until the salmon flakes when tested with a fork. Remove and cover to keep warm.
5. When the farro is tender, add the cherries, currants, spinach, and orange juice; stir and cover. Let stand off the heat for 2 to 3 minutes.
6. Plate the salmon and serve with the farro pilaf.

Nutrition Info:
- Per Serving: Calories: 304 ; Fat: 8 g ;Saturated fat: 2 g;Sodium: 139 mg

Steamed Sole Rolls With Greens

Servings: 4
Cooking Time: 10 Minutes
Ingredients:
- 4 (6-ounce) sole fillets
- 2 teaspoons grated peeled fresh ginger root
- 2 cloves garlic, minced
- 2 teaspoons low-sodium soy sauce
- 1 tablespoon rice wine vinegar
- 1 teaspoon toasted sesame oil
- 2 cups fresh torn spinach leaves
- 1 cup fresh stemmed torn kale
- 1 cup sliced mushrooms
- 2 teaspoons toasted sesame seeds

Directions:
1. Cut the sole fillets in half lengthwise. Sprinkle each piece with some of the ginger root and garlic. Roll up the fillets, ginger root side in. Fasten with a toothpick and set aside.
2. In a small bowl, combine the soy sauce, vinegar, and toasted sesame oil.
3. Bring water to a boil over medium heat in a large shallow saucepan that will hold your steamer.
4. Arrange the spinach leaves and kale in the bottom of the steamer. Add the rolled sole fillets. Add the mushrooms, and sprinkle everything with the soy sauce mixture.

5. Cover and steam for 7 to 11 minutes or until the fish is cooked and flakes when tested with a fork. Remove the toothpicks.
6. To serve, sprinkle with the sesame seeds and serve the fish on top of the wilted greens and mushrooms.

Nutrition Info:
- Per Serving: Calories: 263 ; Fat: 8 g ;Saturated fat: 2 g;Sodium: 247 mg

Tilapia Mint Wraps

Servings: 2
Cooking Time: 15 Min
Ingredients:
- Aluminum foil
- 2 (4 oz) tilapia fillets
- 1 tsp olive oil, divided
- ½ tsp seasoning rub blend, divided
- 4 iceberg lettuce leaves, divided
- 4 tbsp. mint sauce
- 1 tbsp. parsley, finely chopped

Directions:
1. Heat the oven to 425°F gas mark 7. Line a baking sheet with aluminum foil.
2. Place the tilapia fillets on the prepared baking sheet and season with olive oil and the seasoning rub blend.
3. Bake in the oven for 12 to 15 minutes, until the fish is fully cooked and flaky.
4. In the meantime, place the lettuce leaves onto serving plates.
5. When the fish is done, add 1 tbsp. of the mint sauce, ½ tbsp. parsley, and 2 oz of tilapia fillets per lettuce leaf and wrap tightly. Place two wraps on each plate and serve at room temperature.

Nutrition Info:
- Per Serving: Calories: 182 ; Fat: 6 g ;Saturated fat: 1 g ;Sodium: 114mg

Halibut Burgers

Servings: 4
Cooking Time: 35 Min
Ingredients:
- Aluminum foil
- 1 lb. halibut fillets
- ½ tsp Himalayan pink salt, divided
- ¼ tsp ground black pepper
- ½ cup whole wheat breadcrumbs
- 1 large free-range egg
- 1 tbsp. garlic, crushed
- ½ tsp dried dill
- 2 tbsp. avocado oil
- 4 whole wheat buns

Directions:
1. Heat the oven to 400°F gas mark 6. Line a baking sheet with aluminum foil.
2. Place the halibut fillets on the baking sheet and season with ¼ tsp salt and pepper. Bake for 15 to 20 minutes, or until the halibut flakes with a fork. Remove from the oven.
3. Transfer the flesh into a medium-sized mixing bowl, removing any bones.
4. Add the breadcrumbs, egg, garlic, dill and the remaining ¼ tsp salt, mix to combine.
5. Mold the fish mixture into 4 patties.

6. Heat the avocado oil in a large heavy bottom pan over medium heat.
7. Gently place the halibut patties in the pan. Fry for 5 to 6 minutes, until browned, flip, and cook for 3 to 5 minutes, remove from the heat.
8. Place 1 fish patty on each of the 4 buns and serve.

Nutrition Info:
- Per Serving: Calories: 294 ; Fat: 16 g ;Saturated fat: 3 g ;Sodium: 458 mg

Cod And Potatoes

Servings: 4
Ingredients:
- 3 Yukon Gold potatoes
- ¼ cup olive oil
- 1/8 teaspoon white pepper
- 1½ teaspoons dried herbs de Provence, divided
- 4 (4-ounce) cod steaks
- 1 tablespoon butter or margarine
- 2 tablespoons lemon juice

Directions:
1. Preheat oven to 350ºF. Spray a 9″ glass baking dish with nonstick cooking spray. Thinly slice the potatoes. Layer in the baking dish, drizzling each layer with a tablespoon of olive oil, a sprinkle of pepper, and some of the herbs de Provence.
2. Bake for 35–45 minutes or until potatoes are browned on top and tender when pierced with a fork. Arrange cod steaks on top of potatoes. Dot with butter and sprinkle with lemon juice and remaining herbs de Provence.
3. Bake for 15–25 minutes longer or until fish flakes when tested with fork.

Nutrition Info:
- Per Serving: Calories: 362.62 ; Fat:17.28 g ;Saturated fat: 3.88 g ;Sodium: 91.56 mg

Citrus Cod Bake

Servings: 2
Cooking Time: 25 Min
Ingredients:
- 2 tbsp. garlic, crushed
- 1 tbsp. olive oil
- 2 rosemary sprigs, stem removed and finely chopped
- 2 oregano sprigs, finely chopped
- 2 cod fillets, rinsed and patted dry
- ¼ tsp Himalayan pink salt
- ¼ tsp ground black pepper
- 1 lime, cut into 4 round slices
- ½ lemon, wedged

Directions:
1. Heat the oven to 450°F gas mark 8.
2. In a small-sized mixing bowl, add the garlic, olive oil, rosemary, and oregano, mix to combine.
3. Place the cod fillets on a baking sheet and season with salt and pepper.
4. Evenly coat both cod fillets with the garlic and herb mixture. Place 2 lime slices on each fillet. Bake for 18 to 25 minutes, or until the cod fillets are completely cooked.
5. Serve with a lemon wedge.

Nutrition Info:
- Per Serving: Calories: 218 ; Fat:3 g ;Saturated fat: 1 g ;Sodium: 430 mg

Catalán Salmon Tacos

Servings: 4
Cooking Time: 20 Minutes
Ingredients:
- 1 teaspoon olive oil
- 1 (6-ounce) salmon fillet
- 1 teaspoon chili powder
- ½ teaspoon dried oregano leaves
- ⅛ teaspoon black pepper
- 1 small onion, diced
- 2 cloves peeled garlic, minced
- 1 (16-ounce) can low-sodium white beans, rinsed and drained
- 1 tomato, chopped
- 1 cup torn fresh Swiss chard leaves
- 2 tablespoons pine nuts
- 4 corn tortillas, heated

Directions:
1. Add the olive oil to a large nonstick skillet and place over medium heat. Rub the salmon fillet with the chili powder, oregano, and pepper.
2. Add the salmon to the pan, skin side down. Cook for 3 minutes, then turn and cook for 5 minutes longer, or until the fish flakes when tested with a fork. Remove the salmon from the pan, flake, and set aside.
3. Add the onion and garlic to the pan and cook for 2 to 3 minutes, stirring frequently, until softened.
4. Add the beans and mash some of them into the onions. Cook for 1 minute, stirring occasionally.
5. Add the tomato and Swiss chard and cook for another 1 to 2 minutes until the greens start to wilt. Add the pine nuts to the mixture.
6. Make the tacos by adding the bean mixture and the salmon to the corn tortillas, and fold them in half. Serve immediately.

Nutrition Info:
- Per Serving: Calories: 296 ; Fat: 8 g ;Saturated fat: 1 g;Sodium: 63 mg

Roasted Shrimp And Veggies

Servings: 4
Cooking Time: 20 Minutes
Ingredients:
- 1 cup sliced cremini mushrooms
- 2 medium chopped Yukon Gold potatoes, rinsed, unpeeled
- 2 cups broccoli florets
- 3 cloves garlic, sliced
- 1 cup sliced fresh green beans
- 1 cup cauliflower florets
- 2 tablespoons fresh lemon juice
- 2 tablespoons low-sodium vegetable broth
- 1 teaspoon olive oil
- 1 teaspoon dried thyme
- ½ teaspoon dried oregano

- Pinch salt
- ⅛ teaspoon black pepper
- ½ pound medium shrimp, peeled and deveined

Directions:
1. Preheat the oven to 400°F.
2. In a large baking pan, combine the mushrooms, potatoes, broccoli, garlic, green beans, and cauliflower, and toss to coat.
3. In a small bowl, combine the lemon juice, broth, olive oil, thyme, oregano, salt, and pepper and mix well. Drizzle over the vegetables
4. Roast for 15 minutes, then stir.
5. Add the shrimp and distribute evenly.
6. Roast for another 5 minutes or until the shrimp curl and turn pink. Serve immediately.

Nutrition Info:
- Per Serving: Calories:192 ; Fat: 3 g ;Saturated fat: 0 g;Sodium: 116 mg

Sesame-pepper Salmon Kabobs

Servings: 4
Ingredients:
- 1 pound salmon steak
- 2 tablespoons olive oil, divided
- ¼ cup sesame seeds
- 1 teaspoon pepper
- 1 red bell pepper
- 1 yellow bell pepper
- 1 red onion
- 8 cremini mushrooms
- 1/8 teaspoon salt

Directions:
1. Prepare and preheat grill. Cut salmon steak into 1″ pieces, discarding skin and bones. Brush salmon with half of the olive oil.
2. In small bowl, combine sesame seeds and pepper and mix. Press all sides of salmon cubes into the sesame seed mixture.
3. Slice bell peppers into 1″ slices and cut red onion into 8 wedges; trim mushroom stems and leave caps whole. Skewer coated salmon pieces, peppers, onion, and mushrooms on metal skewers. Brush vegetables with remaining olive oil and sprinkle with salt.
4. Grill 6″ from medium coals, turning once during cooking time, until the sesame seeds are very brown and toasted and fish is just done, about 6–8 minutes. Serve immediately.

Nutrition Info:
- Per Serving: Calories:319.33 ; Fat:20.26 g ;Saturated fat: 3.67 g ;Sodium:141.88 mg

Cajun-rubbed Fish

Servings: 4

Ingredients:
- ½ teaspoon black pepper
- ¼ teaspoon cayenne pepper
- ½ teaspoon lemon zest
- ½ teaspoon dried dill weed
- 1/8 teaspoon salt
- 1 tablespoon brown sugar
- 4 (5-ounce) swordfish steaks

Directions:
1. Prepare and preheat grill. In small bowl, combine pepper, cayenne pepper, lemon zest, dill weed, salt, and brown sugar and mix well. Sprinkle onto both sides of the swordfish steaks and rub in. Set aside for 30 minutes.
2. Brush grill with oil. Add swordfish; cook without moving for 4 minutes. Then carefully turn steaks and cook for 2–4 minutes on second side until fish just flakes when tested with fork. Serve immediately.

Nutrition Info:
- Per Serving: Calories: 233.57 ; Fat:7.31 g ;Saturated fat: 2.00 g ;Sodium: 237.08 mg

Baked Halibut In Mustard Sauce

Servings: 4

Ingredients:
- 1 pound halibut fillet Pinch of salt
- 1/8 teaspoon white pepper
- 1 tablespoon lemon juice
- 1 teaspoon orange zest
- 2 tablespoons butter or margarine, melted
- ¼ cup skim milk
- 2 tablespoons Dijon mustard
- 1 slice Honey-Wheat Sesame Bread , crumbled

Directions:
1. Preheat oven to 400°F. Spray a 1-quart baking dish with nonstick cooking spray. Cut fish into serving-size pieces and sprinkle with salt, pepper, and lemon juice.
2. In small bowl, combine melted butter, milk, and mustard, and whisk until blended. Stir in the breadcrumbs. Pour this sauce over the fish.
3. Bake for 20–25 minutes, or until fish flakes when tested with fork and sauce is bubbling. Serve immediately.

Nutrition Info:
- Per Serving: Calories: 219.84 ; Fat:9.38 g ;Saturated fat: 4.30 g ;Sodium: 244.95 mg

Seared Scallops With Fruit

Servings: 3–4

Ingredients:
- 1 pound sea scallops Pinch salt
- 1/8 teaspoon white pepper
- 1 tablespoon olive oil
- 1 tablespoon butter or margarine
- ¼ cup dry white wine
- 2 peaches, sliced
- 1 cup blueberries
- 1 tablespoon lime juice

Directions:
1. Rinse scallops and pat dry. Sprinkle with salt and pepper and set aside.
2. In large skillet, heat olive oil and butter over medium-high heat. Add the scallops and don't move them for 3 minutes. Carefully check to see if the scallops are deep golden brown. If they are, turn and cook for 1–2 minutes on the second side.
3. Remove scallops to serving plate. Add peaches to skillet and brown quickly on one side, about 2 minutes. Turn peaches and add wine to skillet; bring to a boil. Remove from heat and add blueberries. Pour over scallops, sprinkle with lime juice, and serve immediately.

Nutrition Info:
- Per Serving: Calories: 207.89; Fat: 7.36 g ;Saturated fat:2.40 g ;Sodium: 242.16 mg

Salmon With Spicy Mixed Beans

Servings: 4

Cooking Time: 20 Minutes

Ingredients:
- 2 teaspoons olive oil, divided
- 4 (4-ounce) salmon fillets
- Pinch salt
- ⅛ teaspoon black pepper
- 1 onion, diced
- 3 cloves peeled garlic, minced
- 1 jalapeño pepper, seeded and minced
- 1 (16-ounce) can low-sodium mixed beans, rinsed and drained
- 2 tablespoons low-fat plain Greek yogurt
- 2 tablespoons minced fresh cilantro

Directions:
1. Put 1 teaspoon of the olive oil in a large skillet and heat over medium heat.
2. Sprinkle the salmon fillets with the salt and pepper and add to the skillet, skin side down.
3. Cook for 5 minutes, then flip the fillets with a spatula and cook for another 3 to 4 minutes or until the salmon flakes when tested with a fork. Remove the fish to a clean warm plate, and cover with an aluminum foil tent to keep warm.
4. Add the remaining 1 teaspoon of the olive oil to the skillet. Add the onion, garlic, and jalapeño pepper; cook, stirring frequently, for 3 minutes.
5. Add the beans and mash with a fork until desired consistency.
6. Remove the pan from the heat, add the yogurt, and stir until combined.
7. Pile the beans onto a serving platter, top with the fish, and sprinkle with the cilantro. Serve immediately.

Nutrition Info:
- Per Serving: Calories: 293 ; Fat: 10 g ;Saturated fat: 2 g;Sodium: 345 mg

Scallops On Skewers With Lemon

Servings: 4

Ingredients:
- 2 tablespoons lemon juice
- 1 teaspoon grated lemon zest
- 2 teaspoons sesame oil
- 2 tablespoons chili sauce
- 1/8 teaspoon cayenne pepper
- 1 pound sea scallops
- 4 strips low-sodium bacon

Directions:
1. Prepare and preheat grill or broiler. In medium bowl, combine lemon juice, zest, sesame oil, chili sauce, and cayenne pepper and mix well. Add scallops and toss to coat. Let stand for 15 minutes.
2. Make skewers with the scallops and bacon. Thread a skewer through one end of the bacon, then add a scallop. Curve the bacon around the scallop and thread onto the skewer so it surrounds the scallop halfway. Repeat with 3 to 4 more scallops and the bacon slice.
3. Repeat with remaining scallops and bacon. Grill or broil 6″ from heat source for 3–5 minutes per side, until bacon is crisp and scallops are cooked and opaque. Serve immediately.

Nutrition Info:
- Per Serving: Calories:173.65 ; Fat:6.48 g ;Saturated fat: 1.51 g;Sodium:266.64 mg

Almond Snapper With Shrimp Sauce

Servings: 6

Ingredients:
- 1 egg white
- ¼ cup dry breadcrumbs
- 1/3 cup ground almonds
- 1/8 teaspoon salt
- 1/8 teaspoon white pepper
- 6 (4-ounce) red snapper fillets
- 3 tablespoons olive oil, divided
- 1 onion, chopped
- 4 cloves garlic, minced
- 1 red bell pepper, chopped
- ¼ pound small raw shrimp
- 1 tablespoon lemon juice
- ½ cup low-fat sour cream
- ½ teaspoon dried dill weed

Directions:
1. Place egg white in shallow bowl; beat until foamy. On shallow plate, combine breadcrumbs, almonds, salt, and pepper and mix well. Dip fish into egg white, then into crumb mixture, pressing to coat. Let stand on wire rack for 10 minutes.
2. In small saucepan, heat 1 tablespoon olive oil over medium heat. Add onion, garlic, and bell pepper; cook and stir until tender, about 5 minutes. Add shrimp; cook and stir just until shrimp curl and turn pink, about 1–2 minutes. Remove from heat and add lemon juice; set aside.
3. In large saucepan, heat remaining 2 tablespoons olive oil over medium heat. Add coated fish fillets. Cook for 4 minutes on one side, then carefully turn and cook for 2–5 minutes on second side until coating is browned and fish flakes when tested with a fork.
4. While fish is cooking, return saucepan with shrimp to medium heat. Add sour cream and dill weed. Heat, stirring, until mixture is hot.

5. Remove fish from skillet and place on serving plate. Top each with a spoonful of shrimp sauce and serve immediately.

Nutrition Info:
- Per Serving: Calories:272.57 ; Fat:13.80 g ;Saturated fat: 3.09 g;Sodium:216.17 mg

Bluefish With Asian Seasonings

Servings: 4

Ingredients:
- 1¼ pounds bluefish fillets
- 1 tablespoon lime juice
- 2 teaspoons low-sodium soy sauce
- 2 teaspoons grated ginger root
- 3 cloves garlic, minced
- 1 teaspoon sesame oil
- 1 teaspoon Thai chile paste
- 1 tablespoon orange juice
- 1/8 teaspoon white pepper

Directions:
1. Preheat broiler. Place bluefish fillets on a broiler pan. In small bowl, combine all remaining ingredients, being very careful to make sure that the chile paste is evenly distributed in the sauce.
2. Pour sauce over the fillets. Broil 6″ from heat for 6–9 minutes or until fish is opaque and flakes when tested with fork. Serve immediately.

Nutrition Info:
- Per Serving: Calories: 193.98 ; Fat:7.17 g ;Saturated fat: 1.46 g ;Sodium: 181.39 mg

Red Snapper With Fruit Salsa

Servings: 4

Ingredients:
- 1 cup blueberries
- 1 cup chopped watermelon
- 1 jalapeño pepper, minced
- ½ cup chopped tomatoes
- 3 tablespoons olive oil, divided
- 2 tablespoons orange juice
- 1/8 teaspoon salt, divided
- 1/8 teaspoon white pepper
- 4 (4-ounce) red snapper fillets
- 1 lemon, thinly sliced

Directions:
1. Preheat oven to 400ºF. Spray a 9″ glass baking pan with nonstick cooking spray and set aside. In medium bowl, combine blueberries, watermelon, jalapeño pepper, tomatoes, 1 tablespoon olive oil, orange juice, and half of the salt. Mix well and set aside.
2. Arrange fillets in prepared pan. Sprinkle with remaining salt and the white pepper and drizzle with 2 tablespoons olive oil. Top with lemon slices.
3. Bake for 15 to 20 minutes, or until fish is opaque and flesh flakes when tested with fork. Place on serving plate and top with blueberry mixture; serve immediately.

Nutrition Info:
- Per Serving: Calories: 254.40; Fat:12.01 g ;Saturated fat:1.82 g ;Sodium:186.42 mg

Vegetarian Mains Recipes

Vegetarian Mains Recipes

Homestyle Bean Soup

Servings: 6
Cooking Time: 20 Min
Ingredients:
- 6 cups low-sodium vegetable stock
- 2 (15 oz) cans low-sodium kidney beans, drained and rinsed
- 1 (16 oz) can pinto beans, drained and rinsed
- 1 (15 oz) can diced tomatoes with their juices
- ½ tsp Italian seasoning
- 1 cup carrots, finely chopped
- 1 cup celery stalk, finely chopped
- Himalayan pink salt
- Ground black pepper

Directions:
1. In a large-sized stockpot, add the vegetable stock, kidney beans, pinto beans, tomatoes in their juice, Italian seasoning, carrots, and celery, mix to combine.
2. Bring to a simmer over medium heat. Cook for 15 minutes, or until heated through. Remove from the heat and season with salt and pepper to taste. Serve hot.

Nutrition Info:
- Per Serving: Calories: 238 ; Fat: 1 g ;Saturated fat: 0 g ;Sodium: 135 mg

Peanut-butter-banana Skewered Sammies

Servings: 4–6
Ingredients:
- ½ cup natural no-salt peanut butter
- 8 slices Honey-Wheat Sesame Bread
- 2 bananas
- 2 tablespoons lime juice
- 2 tablespoons butter or margarine, softened

Directions:
1. Spread peanut butter on one side of each slice of bread. Slice bananas, and as you work, sprinkle with lime juice. Make sandwiches by putting the bananas on the peanut butter and combining slices.
2. Butter the outsides of the sandwiches. Heat grill and cook sandwiches until bread is crisp and golden brown. Remove from grill, cut into quarters, and skewer on wood or metal skewers. Serve immediately.

Nutrition Info:
- Per Serving: Calories:376.36; Fat:18.67 g ;Saturated fat: 5.57 g ;Sodium: 77.44 mg

Cheese-and-veggie Stuffed Artichokes

Servings: 4

Ingredients:
- 1 cup shredded Havarti cheese
- 2 tablespoons grated Parmesan cheese
- ¼ cup plain yogurt
- ¼ cup low-fat mayonnaise
- 1 tablespoon lemon juice
- 2 scallions, chopped
- 1 tablespoon capers
- 1 cup grated carrots
- 1 cup grape tomatoes
- 1/8 teaspoon salt
- 4 globe artichokes
- 1 lemon, cut into wedges

Directions:
1. In medium bowl, combine Havarti, Parmesan, yogurt, mayonnaise, lemon juice, scallions, and capers and mix well. Stir in carrots, tomatoes, and salt, and set aside.
2. Cut off the top inch of the artichokes. Cut off the sharp tip of each leaf. Pull off the tough outer leaves and discard. Rub cut edges with lemon wedges. Cut artichokes in half lengthwise.
3. Bring a large pot of salted water to a boil and add lemon wedges. Add artichokes and simmer for 20–25 minutes or until a leaf pulls out easily from the artichoke. Cool, then carefully remove choke with spoon.
4. Stuff artichokes with the cheese mixture, place on serving plate, cover, and chill for 2–4 hours before serving.

Nutrition Info:
- Per Serving: Calories: 266.61; Fat:14.24 g ;Saturated fat:6.47 g ;Sodium: 413.37 mg

Roasted Garlic Soufflé

Servings: 4

Ingredients:
- 1 head Roasted Garlic
- 2 tablespoons olive oil
- 1 cup finely chopped cooked turkey breast
- ¼ cup grated Parmesan cheese
- 1/8 teaspoon pepper
- 1 egg
- ¼ cup low-fat sour cream
- 6 egg whites
- ¼ teaspoon cream of tartar
- ¼ cup chopped flat-leaf parsley

Directions:
1. Preheat oven to 375ºF. Grease the bottom of a 2-quart soufflé dish with peanut oil and set aside. Squeeze the garlic from the papery skins. Discard skins, and in medium bowl, combine olive oil with the garlic. Add turkey, cheese, pepper, egg, and sour cream, and mix well.
2. In large bowl, combine egg whites with cream of tartar. Beat until stiff peaks form. Stir a spoonful of egg whites into the turkey mixture and stir well. Then fold in remaining egg whites. Fold in parsley.
3. Spoon mixture into prepared soufflé dish. Bake for 40–50 minutes or until the soufflé is puffed and golden. Serve immediately.

Nutrition Info:
- Per Serving: Calories:223.79 ; Fat: 14.23 g ;Saturated fat:3.92 g ;Sodium: 253.37 mg

Spaghetti With Creamy Tomato Sauce

Servings: 6–8
Ingredients:
- 1 recipe Spaghetti Sauce
- ½ cup fat-free half-and-half
- 1 (16-ounce) package whole-grain pasta
- ½ cup grated Parmesan cheese

Directions:
1. Bring large pot of water to a boil. Prepare Spaghetti Sauce as directed. During last 5 minutes of cooking time, stir in light cream and stir to blend.
2. Cook pasta in boiling water according to package directions until al dente. Drain and add to Spaghetti Sauce; cook and stir for 1 minute to let the pasta absorb some of the sauce. Sprinkle with Parmesan and serve immediately.

Nutrition Info:
- Per Serving: Calories: 354.63; Fat:6.65 g ;Saturated fat:1.90 g ;Sodium:188.68 mg

Salad Sandwich

Servings: 2
Cooking Time: 15 Min
Ingredients:
- 2 tsp apple cider vinegar
- 1 tsp avocado oil
- ¼ tsp ground cumin
- ¼ tsp wholegrain mustard
- ⅓ cup carrot, grated
- 2 tbsp. hummus, divided
- 4 slices wholegrain multigrain bread
- ½ ripe avocado, sliced
- 6 (½-inch-thick) jarred roasted red peppers, drained well
- 4 iceberg lettuce leaves

Directions:
1. In a small-sized mixing bowl, add the apple cider vinegar, avocado oil, cumin, and mustard, whisk to combine. Add the carrot and toss to coat and marinate for 10 minutes.
2. Spread the hummus on each slice of bread.
3. Divide the avocado slices between the two sandwiches. Top with peppers and lettuce.
4. Drain the marinaded carrots and add them on top of the lettuce. Close the sandwiches and enjoy.

Nutrition Info:
- Per Serving: Calories: 384 ; Fat: 16 g ;Saturated fat: 2 g ;Sodium: 463 mg

Chili-sautéed Tofu With Almonds

Servings: X
Cooking Time: 15 Minutes
Ingredients:
- 2 teaspoons olive oil
- ½ jalapeño pepper, chopped
- 1 teaspoon grated fresh ginger
- 1 teaspoon minced garlic
- 12 ounces extra-firm tofu, drained and cut into
- 1-inch cubes
- 2 cups shredded bok choy
- 1 red bell pepper, thinly sliced
- 1 scallion, white and green parts, thinly sliced
- 1 tablespoon low-sodium tamari sauce
- 1 tablespoon freshly squeezed lime juice
- 1 cup cooked quinoa, for serving
- ¼ cup chopped almonds, for garnish

Directions:
1. In a large skillet, warm the olive oil over medium-high heat.
2. Add the jalapeño, ginger, and garlic and sauté until softened, about 4 minutes.
3. Add the tofu, bok choy, bell peppers, and scallions and sauté until the tofu is lightly browned and the vegetables are tender, 8 to 10 minutes.
4. Stir in the tamari sauce and lime juice and toss to coat the ingredients.
5. Serve over quinoa, topped with chopped almonds.

Nutrition Info:
- Per Serving: Calories: 469 ; Fat: 24 g ;Saturated fat: 2 g ;Sodium: 279 mg

Bean And Veggie Cassoulet

Servings: X
Cooking Time: 25 Minutes
Ingredients:
- 1 teaspoon olive oil
- ½ cup chopped sweet onion
- ½ cup chopped celery
- ½ cup shredded carrot
- 1 teaspoon minced garlic
- 1 cup low-sodium canned pinto beans, rinsed and drained
- 1 cup low-sodium canned black beans, rinsed and drained
- 1 cup low-sodium canned lentils, rinsed and drained
- 1 cup low-sodium vegetable broth
- 2 large tomatoes, chopped
- 1 cup shredded Swiss chard or collard greens
- 1 teaspoon chopped fresh oregano
- ½ teaspoon ground coriander
- Sea salt
- Freshly ground black pepper

Directions:
1. In a large saucepan, warm the oil over medium-high heat.
2. Add the onions, celery, carrots, and garlic and sauté until softened, 5 to 7 minutes.

3. Stir in the beans, lentils, and vegetable broth and bring the mixture to a boil. Reduce the heat to low and simmer 10 minutes.
4. Stir in the tomatoes, greens, oregano, and coriander and simmer until the greens are tender, about 5 minutes.
5. Season the cassoulet with salt and pepper and serve.

Nutrition Info:
- Per Serving: Calories: 446 ; Fat:4 g ;Saturated fat: 1 g ;Sodium: 127 mg

Rice-and-vegetable Casserole

Servings: 8
Ingredients:
- 1 tablespoon olive oil
- 2 onions, chopped
- 1 (8-ounce) package sliced mushrooms
- 2 red bell peppers, chopped
- 1 jalapeño pepper, minced
- 4 cups cooked brown rice
- 1½ cups milk
- 1 egg
- 2 egg whites
- ½ cup low-fat sour cream
- 1 cup shredded part-skim mozzarella cheese
- ½ cup shredded Colby cheese

Directions:
1. Preheat oven to 350ºF. Spray a 13″ × 9″ baking pan with nonstick cooking spray and set aside.
2. In large saucepan, heat olive oil. Add onions and mushrooms; cook and stir for 3 minutes. Then add bell peppers and jalapeño pepper; cook and stir for 3–4 minutes longer until vegetables are crisp-tender.
3. In large bowl, combine rice, milk, egg, egg whites, sour cream, mozzarella cheese, and Colby cheese. Layer half of this mixture in the prepared baking pan. Top with vegetables, then top with remaining rice mixture. Bake for 50–65 minutes or until casserole is bubbling, set, and beginning to brown. Let stand for 5 minutes, then cut into squares to serve.

Nutrition Info:
- Per Serving: Calories:276.42; Fat:10.87 g ;Saturated fat:5.35 g ;Sodium: 175.20 mg

Pinto Bean Tortillas

Servings: 4
Cooking Time: 25 Min
Ingredients:
- 1 (15 oz) can low-sodium pinto beans, rinsed and drained
- ¼ cup canned fire-roasted tomato salsa
- ¾ cup dairy-free cheddar cheese, shredded and divided
- 1 medium red bell pepper, seeded, chopped and divided
- 2 tbsp. olive oil, divided
- 4 large, wholegrain tortillas

Directions:
1. Place the drained pinto beans and the tomato salsa together in a food processor. Process until smooth.
2. Spread ½ cup of the pinto bean mixture on each tortilla. Sprinkle each tortilla with 3 tbsp. of dairy-free cheddar cheese and ¼ cup of red bell pepper. Fold in half and repeat with the remaining tortillas.
3. Add 1 tbsp. of olive oil to a large, heavy-bottom pan over medium heat until hot. Place the first two folded tortillas

in the pan. Cover and cook for 2 minutes until the tortillas are crispy on the bottom. Flip and cook for 2 minutes until crispy on the other side.

4. Repeat with the remaining folded tortillas and the remaining olive oil. Keep warm until ready to serve.

Nutrition Info:
- Per Serving: Calories:438 ; Fat: 21 g ;Saturated fat: 5 g ;Sodium: 561 mg

Quinoa-stuffed Peppers

Servings: 6
Ingredients:
- 1 recipe Quinoa Pepper Pilaf
- ½ cup chopped flat-leaf parsley
- 1 cup shredded Havarti cheese
- 6 large red bell peppers
- 2 cups Spaghetti Sauce

Directions:
1. Preheat oven to 350ºF. Prepare pilaf and fluff. Stir in parsley and Havarti. Cut tops from peppers and remove seeds and membranes.
2. Spray 9″ × 13″ baking dish with nonstick cooking spray. Place a layer of Spaghetti Sauce in the dish. Stuff peppers with pilaf and arrange on sauce. Pour remaining sauce over and around peppers.
3. Bake for 50–60 minutes or until peppers are tender. Serve immediately.

Nutrition Info:
- Per Serving: Calories: 406.04 ; Fat:15.40 g ;Saturated fat: 4.69 g ;Sodium: 468.06 mg

Hearty Vegetable Stew

Servings: X
Cooking Time: 25 Minutes
Ingredients:
- 2 teaspoons olive oil
- 2 celery stalks, chopped
- ½ sweet onion, peeled and chopped
- 1 teaspoon minced garlic
- 3 cups low-sodium vegetable broth
- 1 cup chopped tomatoes
- 2 carrots, thinly sliced
- 1 cup cauliflower florets
- 1 cup broccoli florets
- 1 yellow bell pepper, diced
- 1 cup low-sodium canned black beans, rinsed and drained
- Pinch red pepper flakes
- Sea salt
- Freshly ground black pepper
- 2 tablespoons grated low-fat Parmesan cheese, for garnish
- 1 tablespoon chopped fresh parsley, for garnish

Directions:
1. In a large saucepan, warm the olive oil over medium-high heat.
2. Add the celery, onions, and garlic and sauté until softened, about 4 minutes.
3. Stir in the vegetable broth, tomatoes, carrots, cauliflower, broccoli, bell peppers, black beans, and red pepper flakes.
4. Bring the stew to a boil, then reduce the heat to low and simmer until the vegetables are tender, 18 to 20 minutes.

5. Season with salt and pepper.
6. Serve topped with Parmesan cheese and parsley.

Nutrition Info:
- Per Serving: Calories:270 ; Fat: 8g ;Saturated fat: 3g ;Sodium: 237 mg

Spaghetti Sauce

Servings: 6
Ingredients:
- 2 tablespoons olive oil
- 1 onion, chopped
- 4 cloves garlic, minced
- 1 cup chopped celery
- 1 (8-ounce) package sliced mushrooms
- 1 (6-ounce) can no-salt tomato paste
- 2 (14-ounce) cans no-salt diced tomatoes, undrained
- 1 tablespoon dried Italian seasoning
- ½ cup grated carrots
- 1/8 teaspoon white pepper
- ½ cup dry red wine
- ½ cup water

Directions:
1. In large saucepan, heat olive oil over medium heat. Add onion and garlic; cook and stir until crisp-tender, about 4 minutes. Add celery and mushrooms; cook and stir for 2–3 minutes longer.
2. Add tomato paste; let paste brown a bit without stirring (this adds flavor to the sauce). Then add remaining ingredients and stir gently but thoroughly.
3. Bring sauce to a simmer, then reduce heat to low and partially cover. Simmer for 60–70 minutes, stirring occasionally, until sauce is blended and thickened. Serve over hot cooked pasta, couscous, or rice.

Nutrition Info:
- Per Serving: Calories: 155.73; Fat:5.11 g ;Saturated fat:0.72 g ;Sodium: 84.74 mg

Stuffed Noodle Squash

Servings: 4
Cooking Time: 50 Min
Ingredients:
- 2 small spaghetti squash, halved lengthwise and seeds removed
- 1 cup water
- Aluminum foil
- 2 tbsp. olive oil
- 2 cups spinach, stems removed and finely chopped
- 1 cup chayote squash, peeled and chopped
- 1 cup canned garbanzo bean, drained and rinsed
- ¼ tsp fine sea salt
- ¼ tsp ground black pepper
- 1 cup Marinara Sauce

Directions:
1. Heat the oven to 400°F gas mark 6.
2. Place the spaghetti squashes cut side down on a large baking sheet.

3. Add the water to the baking sheet and cover it with aluminum foil. Bake for 35 to 40 minutes, or until the squash is fully cooked. Remove from the oven, leaving the oven on.
4. In a large, heavy-bottom pan, heat the olive oil over a medium heat.
5. Add the spinach and fry for 2 to 3 minutes until wilted.
6. Add the chayote squash and garbanzo beans, cook for 2 minutes until heated through.
7. Use a fork to scrape the flesh from the squash to remove the strands. Keep the shells.
8. Mix the strands into the garbanzo beans mixture and season with salt and pepper. Divide the mixture into the squash shells.
9. Drizzle each shell with ¼ cup Marinara Sauce. Return the stuffed squash to the oven and bake for 10 minutes until heated through. Serve hot.

Nutrition Info:
- Per Serving: Calories: 252 ; Fat: 13 g ;Saturated fat: 2 g ;Sodium: 330 mg

Quinoa Pepper Pilaf

Servings: 6
Ingredients:
- 2 tablespoons olive oil
- 2 Italian frying peppers, chopped
- 1 green bell pepper, chopped
- 1 red bell pepper, chopped
- 1 onion, chopped
- 4 garlic cloves, minced
- ¼ cup chopped sun-dried tomatoes
- 1/8 teaspoon salt
- 1/8 teaspoon white pepper
- 1¼ cups quinoa
- 2½ cups low-sodium vegetable broth

Directions:
1. In large saucepan, heat olive oil over medium heat. Add frying peppers, green bell pepper, red bell pepper, onion, and garlic; cook and stir until crisp-tender, about 4 minutes. Add sun-dried tomatoes, salt, pepper, and quinoa; cook and stir for 2 minutes.
2. Pour in 1½ cups broth and bring to a simmer. Reduce heat to medium low and cook, stirring frequently, until the broth is absorbed, about 7 minutes. Add remaining broth and cook, stirring frequently, until quinoa is tender. Cover and remove from heat; let stand for 5 minutes. Fluff with a fork and serve.

Nutrition Info:
- Per Serving: Calories:241.29; Fat: 8.16 g ;Saturated fat: 1.14 g ;Sodium: 199.17 mg

Corn-and-chili Pancakes

Servings: 6
Ingredients:
- ½ cup buttermilk
- 1 tablespoon olive oil
- ½ cup egg substitute
- ½ cup grated extra-sharp Cheddar cheese
- 1 jalapeño pepper, minced
- 2 ears sweet corn
- ½ cup cornmeal
- 1 cup all-purpose flour

- 1½ teaspoons baking powder
- ½ teaspoon baking soda
- 1 tablespoon sugar
- 1 tablespoon chili powder
- 1 tablespoon peanut oil
- 1 tablespoon butter

Directions:
1. In large bowl, combine buttermilk, olive oil, egg substitute, Cheddar, and jalapeño pepper and mix well.
2. Cut the kernels off the sweet corn and add to buttermilk mixture along with cornmeal, flour, baking powder, baking soda, sugar, and chili powder; mix until combined. Let stand for 10 minutes.
3. Heat griddle or frying pan over medium heat. Brush with the butter, then add the batter, ¼ cup at a time. Cook until bubbles form and start to break and sides look dry, about 3–4 minutes. Carefully flip pancakes and cook until light golden brown on second side, about 2–3 minutes. Serve immediately.

Nutrition Info:
- Per Serving: Calories:252.62; Fat: 9.20 g ;Saturated fat:3.03 g ;Sodium:287.01 mg

Cauliflower, Green Pea, And Wild Rice Pilaf

Servings: X
Cooking Time: 45 Minutes
Ingredients:
- 2 teaspoons olive oil
- ½ small sweet onion, chopped
- 1 teaspoon minced garlic
- 1 cup wild rice
- 3½ cups low-sodium vegetable broth
- 1 cup small cauliflower florets
- 1 cup frozen green peas
- ½ cup low-sodium canned lentils, rinsed and drained
- 1 teaspoon chopped fresh thyme
- 2 tablespoons sunflower seeds

Directions:
1. In a large skillet, warm the olive oil over medium-high heat.
2. Add the onions and garlic and sauté until softened, about 3 minutes.
3. Stir in the rice and broth and bring to a boil. Reduce the heat to low, cover, and let simmer until most of the liquid is absorbed and the rice is tender, about 45 minutes.
4. While the rice is cooking, place a medium saucepan filled with water over high heat and bring to a boil. Add the cauliflower and peas and blanch until tender-crisp, about 5 minutes. Drain and set aside.
5. When the rice is cooked, stir in the lentils, cauliflower, peas, thyme, and sunflower seeds.
6. Serve.

Nutrition Info:
- Per Serving: Calories: 565 ; Fat: 9 g ;Saturated fat: 1 g ;Sodium: 150 mg

Kidney Bean Stew

Servings: 4
Cooking Time: 25 Min
Ingredients:
- 2 tsp avocado oil
- 1 leek, thinly sliced
- ½ brown onion, finely chopped
- 1 tsp garlic, minced
- 3 cups low-sodium vegetable stock
- 1 cup Roma tomatoes, chopped
- 2 medium carrots, peeled and thinly sliced
- 1 cup cauliflower florets
- 1 cup broccoli florets
- 1 green bell pepper, seeds removed and diced
- 1 cup low-sodium canned kidney beans, rinsed and drained
- Pinch red pepper flakes
- Himalayan pink salt
- Ground black pepper
- 2 tbsp. low-fat Parmesan cheese, grated for garnish
- 1 tbsp. parsley, chopped for garnish

Directions:
1. In a large-sized stockpot, warm the avocado oil over medium-high heat.
2. Add the sliced leek, chopped onions, and minced garlic and fry for 4 minutes until softened.
3. Add the vegetable stock, tomatoes, carrots, cauliflower, broccoli, green bell peppers, kidney beans, and red pepper flakes, mix to combine.
4. Bring the stew to a boil, then reduce the heat to low and simmer for 18 to 20 minutes until the vegetables are tender.
5. Season with salt and pepper to taste.
6. Top with Parmesan cheese and parsley.

Nutrition Info:
- Per Serving: Calories:270 ; Fat: 8g ;Saturated fat: 3g ;Sodium: 237 mg

Sesame Soba Noodles

Servings: X
Cooking Time: 10 Minutes
Ingredients:
- 1 (4-ounce) package uncooked soba noodles
- 2 teaspoons sesame oil
- 1 teaspoon minced garlic
- 2 cups broccoli florets
- 1 cup snow peas, stringed
- 1 red bell pepper, thinly sliced
- 1 carrot, thinly sliced
- 1 cup bean sprouts
- ½ teaspoon low-sodium tamari sauce
- ½ scallion, white and green parts, thinly sliced
- 1 tablespoon sesame seeds, for garnish

Directions:
1. Cook the noodles according to the package directions with no added salt or oil. Drain and set aside in a large bowl.
2. In a large skillet, warm the sesame oil over medium-high heat. Add the garlic and sauté for 3 minutes.

3. Add the broccoli, snow peas, bell peppers, and carrots to the skillet and sauté until the vegetables are tender-crisp, 6 to 7 minutes.
4. Add the bean sprouts, tamari, and scallions and sauté for 1 more minute.
5. Add the soba noodles to the skillet and toss to combine.
6. Serve topped with sesame seeds.

Nutrition Info:
- Per Serving: Calories: 384 ; Fat: 8 g ;Saturated fat: 1 g ;Sodium: 358 mg

Pumpkin And Chickpea Patties

Servings: X
Cooking Time: 20 Minutes
Ingredients:
- 2 teaspoons olive oil, divided
- 2 cups grated fresh pumpkin
- ½ cup grated carrot
- ½ teaspoon minced garlic
- 2 cups low-sodium chickpeas, rinsed and drained
- ½ cup ground almonds
- 2 large egg whites
- 1 scallion, white and green parts, chopped
- ½ teaspoon chopped fresh thyme
- Sea salt
- Freshly ground black pepper

Directions:
1. Preheat the oven to 400°F.
2. Line a baking sheet with parchment paper and set aside.
3. In a large skillet, heat ½ teaspoon olive oil over medium-high heat. Add the pumpkin, carrots, and garlic and sauté until softened, about 4 minutes. Remove from the heat and transfer to a food processor. Wipe the skillet clean with paper towels.
4. Add the chickpeas, almonds, egg whites, scallions, and thyme to the food processor. Pulse until the mixture holds together when pressed.
5. Season with salt and pepper and divide the pumpkin mixture into 8 equal patties, flattening them to about ½-inch thick.
6. Heat the remaining 1½ teaspoons olive oil in the skillet. Cook the patties until lightly browned, about 4 minutes on each side.
7. Place the skillet in the oven and bake for an additional 5 minutes, until the patties are completely heated through.
8. Serve.

Nutrition Info:
- Per Serving: Calories: 560 ; Fat: 25 g ;Saturated fat: 3 g ;Sodium: 62 mg

Soups, Salads,
And Sides Recipes

Soups, Salads, And Sides Recipes

Cosmoked Salmon And Turkey Wasabi Wraps

Servings: 12

Ingredients:
- 1 medium cantaloupe
- 1 tablespoon lime juice
- 4 ounces thinly sliced cold-smoked salmon
- 4 ounces thinly sliced smoked turkey
- ½ cup light mayonnaise
- 1 teaspoon wasabi paste

Directions:
1. Peel cantaloupe and remove seeds. Cut cantaloupe in half, then cut each half crosswise into 12 pieces. Sprinkle with lime juice.
2. Arrange salmon slices on work surface. In small bowl, combine mayonnaise with wasabi paste and mix very well with wire whisk. Be sure the wasabi is evenly distributed. Spread over salmon and turkey slices.
3. Wrap one coated salmon slice or turkey slice around a slice of cantaloupe, mayonnaise side in. Serve immediately or cover and refrigerate for 2 hours before serving.

Nutrition Info:
- Per Serving: Calories:75.82 ; Fat: 3.97 g ;Saturated fat: 0.65 g ;Sodium: 385.38 mg

Fennel-and-orange Salad

Servings: 4

Ingredients:
- 2 fresh oranges
- 1 fennel bulb
- 4 scallions, trimmed and finely chopped
- 3 tablespoons olive oil
- 1 teaspoon fennel seeds, crushed
- 2 tablespoons lemon juice
- 1 tablespoon mustard
- 1/8 teaspoon white pepper
- 1 jalapeño pepper, minced, if desired
- 4 cups baby spinach leaves
- ¼ cup sliced almonds, toasted

Directions:
1. Peel the oranges, and slice them thinly crosswise. Set aside. Trim the fennel and remove the outer layer. Using a mandoline or vegetable peeler, shave the fennel into thin ribbons.
2. In small bowl, combine scallions, oil, fennel seeds, lemon juice, mustard, pepper, and jalapeño, if using. Whisk thoroughly until combined.
3. Arrange spinach leaves on chilled salad plates. Top with the orange slices and fennel. Drizzle with dressing, sprinkle with almonds, and serve immediately.

Nutrition Info:
- Per Serving: Calories:193.25 ; Fat:13.54 g ;Saturated fat:1.66 g ;Sodium: 148.69 mg

Yogurt Cheese Balls

Servings: 8

Ingredients:
- 2 cups plain low-fat yogurt
- ¼ cup minced flat-leaf parsley
- ¼ cup minced chives
- 3 tablespoons extra-virgin olive oil
- 1 tablespoon aged balsamic vinegar

Directions:
1. To make the yogurt cheese, the day before, line a strainer with cheesecloth or a coffee filter. Place the strainer in a large bowl and add the yogurt. Cover and refrigerate overnight. The next day, place the thickened yogurt in a medium bowl. Discard the liquid, or whey, or reserve for use in soups and gravies.
2. Roll the yogurt cheese into 1″ balls. On shallow plate, combine parsley and chives. Roll yogurt balls in herbs to coat. Place on serving plate and drizzle with olive oil and vinegar. Serve immediately.

Nutrition Info:
- Per Serving: Calories: 84.35; Fat:6.03 g ;Saturated fat: 1.31 g ;Sodium:44.06 mg

Piquant Navy Beans

Servings: X
Cooking Time: 15 Minutes

Ingredients:
- 1 teaspoon olive oil
- ½ cup chopped sweet onion
- ½ jalapeño pepper, chopped
- 1 teaspoon minced garlic
- 1 (15-ounce) can low-sodium navy beans, rinsed and drained
- ¼ teaspoon ground cumin
- ⅛ teaspoon ground coriander
- Sea salt
- Freshly ground black pepper
- 1 teaspoon chopped fresh cilantro, for garnish

Directions:
1. In a medium saucepan, warm the olive oil over medium-high heat.
2. Add the onions, jalapeños, and garlic and sauté until softened, about 4 minutes.
3. Stir in the beans, cumin, and coriander and sauté until the beans are heated through, about 10 minutes.
4. Season with salt and pepper and serve topped with cilantro.

Nutrition Info:
- Per Serving: Calories: 291 ; Fat: 4 g ;Saturated fat: 1 g ;Sodium: 34 mg

butternut Squash And Lentil Soup

Servings: 4
Cooking Time: 20 Minutes
Ingredients:

- 1 tablespoon olive oil
- 1 onion, chopped
- 1 tablespoon peeled grated fresh ginger root
- 1 (12-ounce) package peeled and diced butternut squash
- 1 cup red lentils, rinsed and sorted
- 5 cups low-sodium vegetable broth
- 1 cup unsweetened apple juice
- Pinch salt
- ⅛ teaspoon black pepper
- ¼ teaspoon curry powder
- 1 sprig fresh thyme
- 3 tablespoons crumbled blue cheese

Directions:

1. In a large saucepan, heat the olive oil over medium heat. Add the onion, and cook and stir for 3 minutes. Add the ginger, squash, and lentils, and cook and stir for 1 minute.
2. Turn up the heat to medium-high, and add the broth, apple juice, salt, pepper, curry powder, and thyme. Bring the mixture to a boil.
3. Reduce the heat to low and partially cover the pan. Simmer for 15 to 18 minutes or until the squash and lentils are tender. Remove the thyme sprig; the leaves will have fallen off.
4. Purée the soup, either in a food processor, with an immersion blender, or with a potato masher. Heat again, then ladle into bowls, sprinkle with the blue cheese, and serve warm.

Nutrition Info:

- Per Serving: Calories: 317 ; Fat: 7g ;Saturated fat: 2g ;Sodium:280 mg

Lemony Green Beans With Almonds

Servings: 5
Cooking Time: 2 Minutes
Ingredients:

- 3 cups water
- 1 pound green beans, trimmed
- 1 cup diced carrots
- 1 red bell pepper, sliced
- ¼ cup slivered almonds
- ½ cup Lemon-Garlic Sauce

Directions:

1. In a medium pot over high heat, bring the water to a boil. Once the water is boiling, add the green beans and cook for 2 minutes, then drain the beans and run under cold water to cool them.
2. In a large bowl, combine the green beans, carrots, bell pepper, almonds, and Lemon-Garlic Sauce. Enjoy.

Nutrition Info:

- Per Serving: Calories: 133 ; Fat: 8 g ;Saturated fat: 1 g ;Sodium: 254 mg

Grilled Vegetable Pasta Salad

Servings: X
Cooking Time: 10 Minutes
Ingredients:

- 1 tablespoon olive oil, divided
- 1 green zucchini, sliced lengthwise into ¼-inch strips
- 1 yellow squash, sliced lengthwise into ¼-inch strips
- 1 red bell pepper, halved and seeded
- ½ small red onion, sliced
- 6 asparagus spears, woody ends trimmed
- 2 cups cooked whole-grain penne pasta
- ½ cup low-sodium canned cannellini beans, rinsed and drained
- ½ cup cherry tomatoes, halved
- 2 tablespoons Sun-Dried Tomato and Kalamata Olive Tapenade
- 1 tablespoon chopped fresh basil

Directions:

1. Preheat the grill to medium heat.
2. In a medium bowl, toss together the olive oil, zucchini, yellow squash, bell peppers, onions, and asparagus until the veggies are coated.
3. Place the vegetables into a grilling basket and grill for about 10 minutes, or until the vegetables are tender and slightly charred. Remove the vegetables from the heat and cool for 10 minutes.
4. Chop everything except the asparagus. Cut the asparagus into 2-inch pieces.
5. Place the vegetables in a medium bowl and stir in the pasta, beans, tomatoes, tapenade, and basil and toss to coat.
6. Serve.

Nutrition Info:

- Per Serving: Calories: 433 ; Fat: 12 g ;Saturated fat: 2 g ;Sodium: 150 mg

Roasted-garlic Corn

Servings: 6
Ingredients:

- 3 cups frozen corn, thawed
- 2 tablespoons olive oil
- 2 shallots, minced
- 1 head Roasted Garlic
- 1/8 teaspoon salt
- 1/8 teaspoon white pepper

Directions:

1. Preheat oven to 425°F. Place corn on paper towels and pat to dry. Place a Silpat liner on a 15″ × 10″ jelly-roll pan. Combine corn, olive oil, and shallots on pan and toss to coat. Spread in even layer.
2. Roast corn for 14–22 minutes, stirring once during cooking time, until kernels begin to turn light golden brown in spots.
3. Remove cloves from Roasted Garlic and add to corn along with salt and white pepper. Stir to mix, then serve.

Nutrition Info:

- Per Serving: Calories:147.64 ; Fat: 6.70 g ;Saturated fat: 0.94 g;Sodium: 79.60 mg

Rocket & Goat Cheese

Servings: 4
Cooking Time: 35 Min
Ingredients:

- 3-4 medium beets
- Aluminum foil
- 1 (8 oz) bag rocket
- ¼ cup lite balsamic vinaigrette
- ¼ cup walnuts, chopped
- ¼ cup goat cheese, crumbled

Directions:

1. Heat the oven to 350°F gas mark 4.
2. Scrub the beets well under running water and wrap them in aluminum foil.
3. Place the beets in the oven and bake for 25 to 30 minutes, or until a fork goes in easily. Remove from the oven and cool.
4. Use your hands to remove the skin off the beets, discard the skin. Cut the beets into chunks.
5. Place the beet chunks in a large serving bowl and add the rocket. Drizzle with the balsamic vinaigrette, toss gently.
6. Top with walnuts and goat cheese.

Nutrition Info:

- Per Serving: Calories: 197 ; Fat: 14g;Saturated fat: 2g ;Sodium:171 mg

Sautéed Fennel With Lemon

Servings: 4
Ingredients:

- 2 fennel bulbs
- 2 tablespoons olive oil
- 1 lemon, sliced
- 1/8 teaspoon salt
- 1/8 teaspoon pepper
- 2 tablespoons water
- 2 tablespoons lemon juice

Directions:

1. Trim fronds and ends from fennel bulbs and remove outer layer. Cut the bulb into quarters lengthwise.
2. Heat olive oil in large pan over medium heat. Add fennel and sauté, stirring occasionally, for 5 minutes. Add sliced lemon, salt, pepper, water, and lemon juice. Bring to a simmer, then cover, and simmer over low heat for 10 minutes until fennel is tender. Serve immediately.

Nutrition Info:

- Per Serving: Calories: 116.59; Fat:7.06 g ;Saturated fat: 0.94 g;Sodium: 135.07 mg

Beans For Soup

Servings: 10

Ingredients:
- 1 pound dried beans Water

Directions:
1. Sort beans, then rinse well and drain. Combine in a large pot with water to cover by 1″. Bring to a boil over high heat, then cover pan, remove from heat, and let stand for 2 hours.
2. Place pot in refrigerator and let beans soak overnight. In the morning, drain beans and rinse; drain again. Place in 5- to 6-quart slow cooker with water to just cover. Cover and cook on low for 8–10 hours until beans are tender. Do not add salt or any other ingredient.
3. Package beans in 1-cup portions into freezer bags, including a bit of the cooking liquid in each bag. Seal, label, and freeze for up to 3 months. To use, defrost in refrigerator overnight, or open bag and microwave on defrost until beans begin thawing, then stir into soup to heat.

Nutrition Info:
- Per Serving: Calories: 219.48; Fat:0.16 g ;Saturated fat: 0.03 g ;Sodium: 7.08 mg

Greek Quesadillas

Servings: 8

Ingredients:
- 1 cucumber
- 1 cup plain yogurt
- ½ teaspoon dried oregano leaves
- 1 tablespoon lemon juice
- ½ cup crumbled feta cheese
- 4 green onions, chopped
- 3 plum tomatoes, chopped
- 1 cup fresh baby spinach leaves
- 1 cup shredded part-skim mozzarella cheese
- 12 (6-inch) no-salt corn tortillas

Directions:
1. Peel cucumber, remove seeds, and chop. In small bowl, combine cucumber with yogurt, oregano, and lemon juice and set aside.
2. In medium bowl, combine feta cheese, green onions, tomatoes, baby spinach, and mozzarella cheese and mix well.
3. Preheat griddle or skillet. Place six tortillas on work surface. Divide tomato mixture among them. Top with remaining tortillas and press down gently.
4. Cook quesadillas, pressing down occasionally with spatula, until tortillas are lightly browned. Flip quesadillas and cook on second side until tortillas are crisp and cheese is melted. Cut quesadillas in quarters and serve with yogurt mixture.

Nutrition Info:
- Per Serving: Calories:181.26 ; Fat: 6.34 g ;Saturated fat:3.62 g ;Sodium: 208.14 mg

Tangy Fish And Tofu Soup

Servings: 5
Cooking Time: 10 Minutes
Ingredients:
- 1 pound white fish (such as tilapia), thinly sliced
- ⅓ cup Tangy Soy Sauce
- 8 cups water
- 4 cups chopped napa cabbage
- 1 white onion, chopped
- 12 ounces soft tofu, cubed

Directions:
1. Place the fish and the Tangy Soy Sauce in a resealable plastic bag. Place the bag in the refrigerator and let the fish marinate for 30 minutes.
2. Once marinated, bring the water to a boil in a large pot over high heat. Add the cabbage and onion and bring to a boil again.
3. Add the tofu, marinated fish, and any remaining marinade to the pot.
4. Bring the soup back to a boil, reduce the heat to medium, and simmer for 5 minutes, until fragrant. Serve immediately.

Nutrition Info:
- Per Serving: Calories :181 ; Fat: 4g ;Saturated fat: 1g ;Sodium: 271 mg

Scalloped Potatoes With Aromatic Vegetables

Servings: 8
Ingredients:
- 2 carrots, peeled and sliced
- 2 parsnips, peeled and sliced
- 3 russet potatoes, sliced
- ¼ cup olive oil
- 1/8 teaspoon salt
- 1/8 teaspoon white pepper
- 1 onion, finely chopped
- 4 cloves garlic, minced
- 1/3 cup grated Parmesan cheese
- ¼ cup dry breadcrumbs
- 1 cup milk

Directions:
1. Preheat oven to 375ºF. Spray a 9″ × 13″ baking dish with nonstick cooking spray and set aside.
2. In large bowl, combine carrots, parsnips, and potatoes; drizzle with olive oil, sprinkle with salt and pepper, and toss to coat. Layer vegetables in prepared baking dish, sprinkling each layer with onion, garlic, Parmesan, and breadcrumbs, finishing with breadcrumbs.
3. Pour milk into casserole. Cover tightly with foil. Bake for 45 minutes, then uncover. Bake for 15–25 minutes longer or until vegetables are tender and top is browned. Serve immediately.

Nutrition Info:
- Per Serving: Calories:271.60 ; Fat:9.04 g ;Saturated fat: 2.03 g;Sodium: 211.64 mg

Sesame-roasted Vegetables

Servings: 6

Ingredients:
- 2 red bell peppers, sliced
- 4 carrots, sliced
- 1½ pounds tiny fingerling potatoes, cut in half lengthwise
- 2 yellow summer squash, sliced
- 2 tablespoons olive oil
- 2 tablespoons honey
- ¼ cup sesame seeds
- 1/8 teaspoon white pepper

Directions:
1. Preheat oven to 400ºF. Place all vegetables in large roasting pan.
2. In small bowl, combine olive oil and honey and mix well. Drizzle over vegetables and toss to coat. Arrange in single layer in pan and sprinkle with sesame seeds and pepper.
3. Roast for 25–35 minutes or until vegetables are tender and sesame seeds are toasted. Serve immediately.

Nutrition Info:
- Per Serving: Calories:257.08; Fat: 8.95 g ;Saturated fat:1.32 g;Sodium:51.01 mg

Legume Chili

Servings: 2

Cooking Time: 30 Min

Ingredients:
- 1 tsp coconut oil
- 1 medium red bell pepper, diced
- ¼ cup brown onion, chopped
- 1 tsp garlic, crushed
- 2 tbsp. chili powder
- 1 tsp paprika
- 1 cup low-sodium canned kidney beans, rinsed and drained
- 1 cup low-sodium canned lentils, rinsed and drained
- 1 cup sugar snap peas
- 1 cup low-sodium canned diced tomatoes, drained
- ½ cup whole kernel corn
- ½ ripe avocado, diced for garnish

Directions:
1. In a large-sized stockpot, warm the coconut oil over medium-high heat.
2. Add the red bell pepper, onions, and garlic and fry for 4 minutes until softened. Stir in the chili powder and paprika and fry for 1 minute.
3. Mix in the kidney beans, lentils, sugar snap peas, tomatoes, and corn and lower the heat to medium. Cook for 25 minutes, stirring occasionally until the chili is fragrant.
4. Serve into bowls and top with avocado.

Nutrition Info:
- Per Serving: Calories: 512 ; Fat: 16g ;Saturated fat: 2 g ;Sodium: 105 mg

Chunky Irish Potato-leek Soup

Servings: 6
Ingredients:
- 3 tablespoons olive oil
- 2 leeks, sliced 2 onions, chopped
- 2 tablespoons flour
- 3 cups Low-Sodium Chicken Broth
- 1 cup water 6 Yukon Gold potatoes, chopped
- 1/8 teaspoon cayenne pepper
- 1 cup 1% milk
- 1 cup fat-free half-and-half
- ¼ teaspoon nutmeg
- 1 bunch chives, minced
- ¼ cup chopped parsley

Directions:
1. In a large soup pot, heat olive oil over medium heat and add sliced leeks and onion. Cook and stir for 5 minutes.
2. Blend in flour; cook and stir for 3 minutes until bubbly. Add broth, water, and potatoes. Bring to a simmer, then reduce heat to low, cover, and simmer for 15–20 minutes or until potatoes are tender. Mash some of the potatoes with a potato masher, leaving some whole.
3. Stir in cayenne pepper, milk, half-and-half, and nutmeg and heat until soup steams. Add chives and parsley and serve immediately.

Nutrition Info:
- Per Serving: Calories:367.19; Fat: 10.70g ;Saturated fat: 3.10 g ;Sodium: 316.15 mg

Low-sodium Chicken Broth

Servings: 8
Ingredients:
- 2 tablespoons olive oil
- 3 pounds cut-up chicken
- 2 onions, chopped
- 5 cloves garlic, minced
- 4 carrots, sliced
- 4 stalks celery, sliced
- 1 tablespoon peppercorns
- 1 bay leaf
- 6 cups water
- 2 tablespoons lemon juice

Directions:
1. In large skillet, heat olive oil over medium heat. Add chicken, skin-side down, and cook until browned, about 8–10 minutes. Place chicken in 5- to 6-quart slow cooker.
2. Add onions and garlic to drippings in skillet; cook and stir for 2–3 minutes, scraping bottom of skillet. Add to slow cooker along with remaining ingredients except lemon juice. Cover and cook on low for 8–9 hours.
3. Strain broth into large bowl. Remove meat from chicken; refrigerate or freeze for another use. Cover broth and refrigerate overnight. In the morning, remove fat solidified on surface and discard. Stir in lemon juice. Pour broth into freezer containers, seal, label, and freeze up to 3 months. To use, defrost in refrigerator overnight.

Nutrition Info:
- Per Serving: Calories: 82.89 ; Fat: 5.22g ;Saturated fat:0.92 mg;Sodium: 39.09 mg

Chili Fries

Servings: 4–6

Ingredients:
- 4 russet potatoes
- 2 tablespoons olive oil
- 2 tablespoons chili powder
- 1 tablespoon grill seasoning
- 1 teaspoon ground cumin
- 1 teaspoon paprika
- ¼ teaspoon pepper

Directions:
1. Preheat oven to 425°F. Scrub potatoes and pat dry; cut into ½" strips, leaving skin on. A few strips won't have any skin. Toss with olive oil and arrange in single layer on a large cookie sheet.
2. In small bowl, combine remaining ingredients and mix well. Sprinkle over potatoes and toss to coat. Arrange in single layer.
3. Bake for 35–45 minutes, turning once during baking time, until potatoes are deep golden brown and crisp. Serve immediately.

Nutrition Info:
- Per Serving: Calories:225.16; Fat: 4.76 g ;Saturated fat: 0.69 g;Sodium: 213.81 mg

Spring Asparagus Soup

Servings: 4

Ingredients:
- 1 tablespoon olive oil
- 3 scallions, chopped
- ½ cup finely chopped sweet onion
- 1 clove garlic, minced
- 2 new potatoes, peeled and chopped
- 1 pound asparagus
- 4 cups Low-Sodium Chicken Broth
- 1 tablespoon lemon juice
- 1 teaspoon lemon zest
- 1 tablespoon fresh thyme leaves
- 1/8 teaspoon white pepper
- 1 cup fat-free half-and-half

Directions:
1. In large soup pot, heat olive oil over medium heat. Add scallions, sweet onion, and garlic; cook and stir for 3 minutes. Then add potatoes; cook and stir for 5 minutes longer.
2. Snap the asparagus spears and discard ends. Chop asparagus into 1" pieces and add to pot along with broth. Bring to a boil, reduce heat, cover, and simmer for 10 minutes.
3. Using an immersion blender, puree the soup until smooth. Add lemon juice, lemon zest, thyme, pepper, and half-and-half, heat until steaming, and serve. You can also serve this soup chilled. (Without an immersion blender, puree the soup in four batches in a blender or food processor, then return to the pot and continue with the recipe.)

Nutrition Info:
- Per Serving: Calories:201.50 ; Fat: 6.04 g ;Saturated fat:1.52 g ;Sodium: 182.69 mg

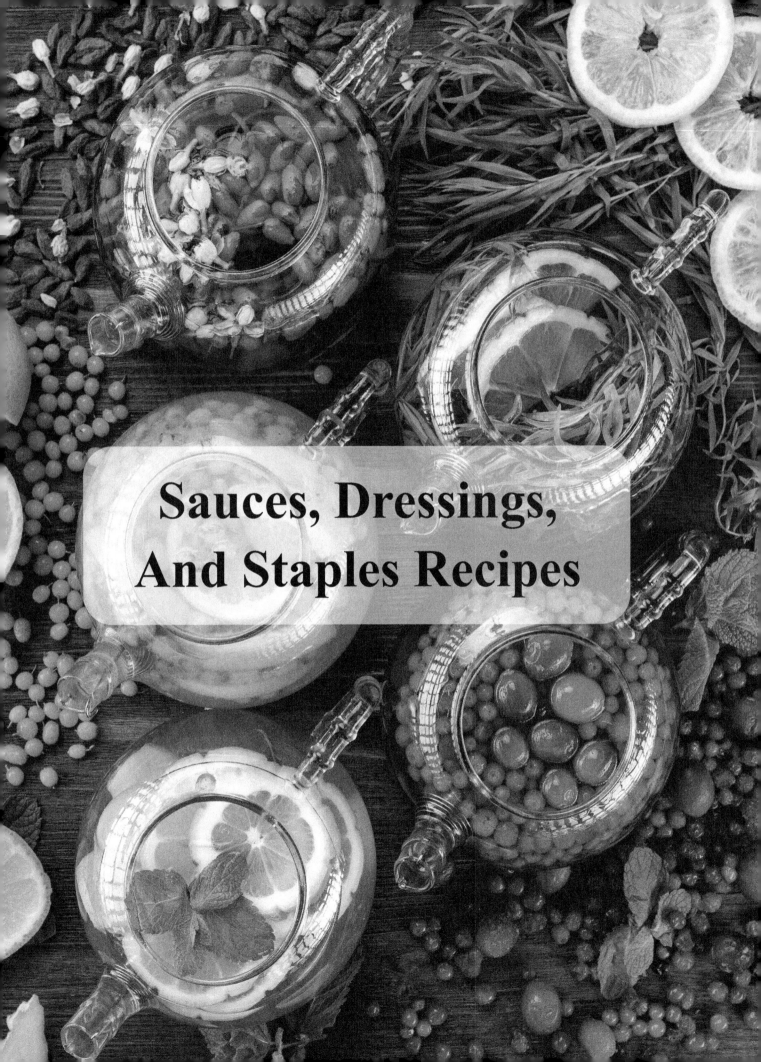

Sauces, Dressings, And Staples Recipes

Sauces, Dressings, And Staples Recipes

Fresh Lime Salsa

Servings: 5
Ingredients:
- 3 tomatoes, coarsely chopped
- ¼ cup chopped white onion
- ¼ cup chopped fresh cilantro
- 1 tablespoon minced garlic
- 1 tablespoon freshly squeezed lime juice
- Sea salt

Directions:
1. In a blender, place the tomatoes, onion, cilantro, garlic, and lime juice and blend until smooth. Season with salt and use immediately.

Nutrition Info:
- Per Serving: Calories: 20; Fat: 0 g ;Saturated fat: 0 g ;Sodium: 36 mg

Silken Fruited Tofu Cream

Servings: 4
Cooking Time: 15 Minutes
Ingredients:
- 1 cup silken tofu
- ⅓ cup fresh raspberries
- 2 tablespoons orange-pineapple juice
- 1 tablespoon fresh lemon juice
- ½ teaspoon vanilla extract
- ⅛ teaspoon ground cinnamon
- Pinch salt

Directions:
1. In a blender or food processor, combine the tofu, raspberries, orange-pineapple juice, lemon juice, vanilla, cinnamon, and salt. Blend or process until smooth.
2. You can use this cream immediately or store it in an airtight glass container in the refrigerator for up to 2 days.

Nutrition Info:
- Per Serving: Calories: 49 ; Fat: 2 g ;Saturated fat: 0 g ;Sodium: 23 mg

Smoky Barbecue Rub

Servings: ½

Ingredients:

- 2 tablespoons smoked paprika
- 2 tablespoons brown sugar
- 1 tablespoon chili powder
- 1 tablespoon garlic powder
- 2 teaspoons onion powder
- 2 teaspoons celery salt
- 1 teaspoon ground cumin
- ½ teaspoon sea salt
- ½ teaspoon dried oregano

Directions:

1. In a small bowl, whisk together the paprika, sugar, chili powder, garlic powder, onion powder, celery salt, cumin, salt, and oregano until well blended.
2. Transfer to an airtight container to store.

Nutrition Info:

- Per Serving: Calories: 23 ; Fat: 1 g ;Saturated fat: 0 g ;Sodium: 113 mg

Chimichurri Rub

Servings: ½

Ingredients:

- 2 tablespoons dried parsley
- 2 tablespoons dried basil
- 1 tablespoon hot paprika
- 1 tablespoon dried oregano
- 2 teaspoons garlic powder
- 1 teaspoon dried thyme
- 1 teaspoon onion powder
- ½ teaspoon freshly ground black pepper
- ¼ teaspoon sea salt
- Pinch red pepper flakes

Directions:

1. In a small bowl, whisk together the parsley, basil, paprika, oregano, garlic powder, thyme, onion powder, pepper, salt, and red pepper flakes until well blended.
2. Transfer to an airtight container to store.

Nutrition Info:

- Per Serving: Calories: 18 ; Fat: 0 g ;Saturated fat: 0 g ;Sodium: 90 mg

Double Tomato Sauce

Servings: 3
Cooking Time: 35 Minutes
Ingredients:
- 1 teaspoon olive oil
- ½ sweet onion, chopped
- 2 teaspoons minced garlic
- 1 (28-ounce) can low-sodium diced tomatoes with their juices
- ½ cup chopped sun-dried tomatoes
- Pinch red pepper flakes
- 2 tablespoons chopped fresh basil
- 2 tablespoons chopped fresh parsley
- Sea salt
- Freshly ground black pepper
- Whole-grain pasta or zucchini noodles, for serving (optional)

Directions:
1. In a large saucepan, warm the olive oil over medium-high heat.
2. Add the onions and garlic and sauté until softened, about 3 minutes.
3. Stir in the tomatoes, sun-dried tomatoes, and red pepper flakes and bring the sauce to a simmer.
4. Reduce the heat and simmer for 20 to 25 minutes.
5. Stir in the basil and parsley and simmer for 5 more minutes.
6. Season with salt and pepper.
7. Serve over whole-grain pasta or zucchini noodles.

Nutrition Info:
- Per Serving: Calories:94 ; Fat: 1 g ;Saturated fat: 0 g ;Sodium: 243mg

Green Sauce

Servings: 4
Cooking Time: 15 Minutes
Ingredients:
- 1 cup watercress
- ½ cup frozen baby peas, thawed
- ¼ cup chopped fresh cilantro leaves
- 2 scallions, chopped
- 3 tablespoons silken tofu
- 2 tablespoons fresh lime juice
- 1 tablespoon green olive slices
- 1 teaspoon grated fresh lime zest
- Pinch salt
- Pinch white pepper

Directions:
1. In a food processor or blender, combine the watercress, peas, cilantro, scallions, tofu, lime juice, olives, lime zest, salt, and white pepper, and process or blend until smooth.
2. This sauce can be used immediately, or you can store it in an airtight glass container in the refrigerator up to four days.

Nutrition Info:
- Per Serving: Calories: 27 ; Fat: 1 g ;Saturated fat: 0 g ;Sodium: 65 mg

Zesty Citrus Kefir Dressing

Servings: 8
Cooking Time: 15 Minutes
Ingredients:
- ⅔ cup kefir
- 2 tablespoons honey
- 2 tablespoons low-sodium yellow mustard
- 2 tablespoons fresh lemon juice
- ½ teaspoon fresh lemon zest
- 1 tablespoon fresh orange juice
- ½ teaspoon fresh orange zest
- 1 teaspoon olive oil
- Pinch salt

Directions:
1. In a blender or food processor, combine the kefir, honey, mustard, lemon juice and zest, orange juice and zest, olive oil, and salt. Blend or process until smooth.
2. You can serve this dressing immediately, or store it in an airtight container in the refrigerator for up to 3 days.

Nutrition Info:
- Per Serving: Calories: 37 ; Fat: 1 g ;Saturated fat: 0 g ;Sodium: 43 mg

Sun-dried Tomato And Kalamata Olive Tapenade

Servings: 1¼
Ingredients:
- ½ cup chopped sun-dried tomatoes
- ½ cup packed fresh basil leaves
- ¼ cup sliced Kalamata olives
- ¼ cup Parmesan cheese
- 2 garlic cloves
- 1 tablespoon olive oil
- Sea salt
- Freshly ground black pepper

Directions:
1. In a food processor or blender, place the sun-dried tomatoes, basil, olives, Parmesan cheese, garlic, and olive oil and pulse until smooth.
2. Season with salt and pepper.

Nutrition Info:
- Per Serving: Calories: 57 ; Fat: 3 g ;Saturated fat: 1 g ;Sodium: 207 mg

Chimichurri Sauce

Servings: 8
Cooking Time: 15 Minutes
Ingredients:

- 1 shallot, chopped
- 1 garlic clove, chopped
- ½ cup fresh flat-leaf parsley
- ½ cup fresh cilantro leaves
- 3 tablespoons fresh basil leaves
- 2 tablespoons fresh lemon juice
- 2 tablespoons low-sodium vegetable broth
- Pinch salt
- ⅛ teaspoon red pepper flakes

Directions:

1. In a blender or food processor, add the shallot, garlic, parsley, cilantro, basil, lemon juice, vegetable broth, salt, and red pepper flakes, and process until the herbs are in tiny pieces and the mixture is well-combined.
2. Serve immediately or store in an airtight glass container in the refrigerator up to 2 days. Stir the sauce before serving.

Nutrition Info:

- Per Serving: Calories: 5 ; Fat: 0 g ;Saturated fat: 0 g ;Sodium: 3 mg

Oregano-thyme Sauce

Servings: 5
Ingredients:

- 2 tablespoons balsamic vinegar
- 1 tablespoon dried oregano
- 1 tablespoon dried thyme
- 1 tablespoon minced garlic
- ½ teaspoon salt

Directions:

1. In a small bowl, mix the vinegar, oregano, thyme, garlic, and salt until well blended. Use immediately

Nutrition Info:

- Per Serving: Calories: 10 ; Fat: 0 g ;Saturated fat: 0 g ;Sodium: 235 mg

Tzatziki

Servings: 4
Ingredients:

- 1¼ cups plain low-fat Greek yogurt
- 1 cucumber, peeled, seeded, and diced
- 2 tablespoons fresh lime juice
- ½ teaspoon grated fresh lime zest
- 2 cloves garlic, minced
- Pinch salt
- ⅛ teaspoon white pepper
- 1 tablespoon minced fresh dill
- 1 tablespoon minced fresh mint
- 2 teaspoons olive oil

Directions:

1. In a medium bowl, combine the yogurt, cucumber, lime juice, lime zest, garlic, salt, white pepper, dill, and mint.
2. Transfer the mixture to a serving bowl. Drizzle with the olive oil.
3. Serve immediately or store in an airtight glass container and refrigerate for up to 2 days

Nutrition Info:

- Per Serving: Calories: 100 ; Fat: 4 g ;Saturated fat: 1 g ;Sodium: 56 mg

Mustard Berry Vinaigrette

Servings: 8
Cooking Time: 10 Minutes
Ingredients:

- 3 tablespoons low-sodium yellow mustard
- ½ cup fresh raspberries
- ½ cup sliced fresh strawberries
- 2 tablespoons raspberry vinegar
- 2 teaspoons agave nectar
- Pinch salt

Directions:

1. In a blender or food processor, combine the mustard, raspberries, strawberries, raspberry vinegar, agave nectar, and salt, and blend or process until smooth. You can also combine the ingredients in a bowl and mash them with the back of a fork.
2. Store the vinaigrette in an airtight glass container in the refrigerator for up to 3 days.

Nutrition Info:

- Per Serving: Calories: 27 ; Fat: 1 g ;Saturated fat: 0 g ;Sodium: 65 mg

Tofu-horseradish Sauce

Servings: X
Ingredients:

- ¼ cup silken tofu
- 1 tablespoon prepared horseradish
- 1 tablespoon minced scallion, white part only
- 1 tablespoon chopped fresh parsley
- ½ teaspoon minced garlic
- Sea salt
- Freshly ground black pepper

Directions:

1. In a small bowl, stir together the tofu, horseradish, scallions, parsley, and garlic until well mixed.
2. Season with salt and pepper.
3. Serve immediately.

Nutrition Info:

- Per Serving: Calories: 20 ; Fat: 0 g ;Saturated fat: 0 g ;Sodium: 50 mg

Cheesy Spinach Dip

Servings: 1½
Cooking Time: 25 Minutes
Ingredients:
- 1 cup thawed chopped frozen spinach
- ½ cup fat-free cottage cheese
- 2 tablespoons chopped sweet onion
- ¼ cup grated Parmesan cheese
- 1 teaspoon minced garlic
- Sea salt
- Freshly ground black pepper

Directions:
1. In a medium bowl, stir together the spinach, cottage cheese, onion, Parmesan cheese, and garlic until well combined.
2. Season with salt and pepper.
3. Place the dip, covered, in the refrigerator until you are ready to serve it.
4. Serve with vegetables or pita bread.

Nutrition Info:
- Per Serving: Calories: 79 ; Fat: 2 g ;Saturated fat: 1 g ;Sodium: 213 mg

Spicy Peanut Sauce

Servings: 8
Cooking Time: 15 Minutes
Ingredients:
- ½ cup powdered peanut butter (see Ingredient Tip)
- 2 tablespoons reduced-fat peanut butter
- ⅓ cup plain nonfat Greek yogurt
- 2 tablespoons fresh lime juice
- 2 teaspoons low-sodium soy sauce
- 1 scallion, chopped
- 1 clove garlic, minced
- 1 jalapeño pepper, seeded and minced
- ⅛ teaspoon red pepper flakes

Directions:
1. In a blender or food processor, combine powdered peanut butter, reduced-fat peanut butter, yogurt, lime juice, soy sauce, scallion, garlic, jalapeño pepper, and red pepper flakes, and blend or process until smooth.
2. Serve immediately or store in an airtight glass container and refrigerate for up to 3 days. You can thin this sauce with more lime juice if necessary.

Nutrition Info:
- Per Serving: Calories: 60 ; Fat: 3 g ;Saturated fat: 0 g ;Sodium: 88 mg

Classic Italian Tomato Sauce

Servings: 4
Cooking Time: 20 Minutes
Ingredients:

- 2 teaspoons olive oil
- 1 onion, chopped
- 3 cloves garlic, minced
- 1½ pounds plum (Roma) tomatoes, chopped
- 2 tablespoons no-salt-added tomato paste
- 2 tablespoons finely grated carrot
- 1 teaspoon dried basil leaves
- ½ teaspoon dried oregano
- ⅛ teaspoon white pepper
- Pinch salt
- Pinch sugar
- 2 tablespoons fresh basil leaves, chopped

Directions:

1. In a large saucepan, heat the olive oil over medium heat.
2. Add the onion and garlic, and cook and stir for 3 minutes or until the onions are translucent.
3. Add the tomatoes, tomato paste, carrot, basil, oregano, white pepper, salt, and sugar, and stir and bring to a simmer.
4. Simmer for 15 to 18 minutes, stirring frequently, or until the sauce thickens slightly.
5. Stir in the fresh basil and serve.

Nutrition Info:

- Per Serving: Calories: 73 ; Fat: 3 g ;Saturated fat: 0 g ;Sodium: 19 mg

Avocado Dressing

Servings: 8
Cooking Time: 15 Minutes
Ingredients:

- 1 avocado, peeled and cubed
- ⅔ cup plain nonfat Greek yogurt
- ¼ cup buttermilk
- 2 tablespoons fresh lemon juice
- 1 tablespoon honey
- Pinch salt
- 2 tablespoons chopped fresh chives
- ½ cup chopped cherry tomatoes

Directions:

1. In a blender or food processor, combine the avocado, yogurt, buttermilk, lemon juice, honey, salt, and chives, and blend or process until smooth. Stir in the tomatoes.
2. You may need to add more buttermilk or lemon juice to achieve a pourable consistency.
3. This dressing can be stored by putting it into a small dish, then pouring about 2 teaspoons lemon juice on top. Cover the dressing by pressing plastic wrap directly onto the surface. Refrigerate for up to 1 day.

Nutrition Info:

- Per Serving: Calories:55 ; Fat: 3g ;Saturated fat: 1g ;Sodium: 30mg

Spinach And Walnut Pesto

Servings: 5

Ingredients:
- 2 cups spinach
- ½ cup chopped walnuts
- ½ cup olive oil
- 2 tablespoons minced garlic
- ½ teaspoon salt

Directions:
1. In a blender, place the spinach, walnuts, olive oil, garlic, and salt and blend until smooth. Use immediately.

Nutrition Info:
- Per Serving: Calories: 275 ; Fat: 29 g ;Saturated fat: 4g ;Sodium: 243 mg

Lemon-garlic Sauce

Servings: 5

Ingredients:
- ¼ cup freshly squeezed lemon juice
- 2 tablespoons olive oil
- 1 tablespoon minced garlic
- 1 tablespoon dried oregano
- ½ teaspoon salt

Directions:
1. In a small bowl, mix the lemon juice, olive oil, garlic, oregano, and salt until well blended. Use immediately.

Nutrition Info:
- Per Serving: Calories: 55 ; Fat: 5 g ;Saturated fat: 1 g ;Sodium: 233 mg

Spicy Honey Sauce

Servings: 5

Ingredients:
- 2 tablespoons vegetable oil
- 1½ tablespoons honey
- 1 tablespoon minced garlic
- 1 tablespoon chili powder
- ½ teaspoon salt

Directions:
1. In a small bowl, mix the vegetable oil, honey, garlic, chili powder, and salt until well blended. Use immediately.

Nutrition Info:
- Per Serving: Calories: 78 ; Fat: 6 g ;Saturated fat: 0 g ;Sodium: 279 mg

Desserts And Treats Recipes

Desserts And Treats Recipes

Banana-rum Mousse

Servings: 4
Ingredients:
- 3 tablespoons rum
- 2 tablespoons lime juice
- 2 tablespoons powdered sugar
- 2 bananas, chopped
- 1 cup vanilla frozen yogurt
- 4 sprigs fresh mint

Directions:
1. In blender or food processor, combine the rum, lime juice, sugar, and bananas and blend or process until smooth.
2. Add the yogurt and blend or process until smooth, scraping down sides once during blending. Spoon into dessert glasses and serve immediately, or cover and freeze up to 8 hours before serving.

Nutrition Info:
- Per Serving: Calories:164.58 ; Fat: 2.25 g ;Saturated fat: 1.13 g;Sodium:32.30 mg

Strawberry-apple-lemon Smoothie Pops

Servings: 7
Ingredients:
- 2 cups strawberries, stems removed
- 1 cup unsweetened apple juice
- 1 tablespoon freshly squeezed lemon juice
- 1 tablespoon honey
- 1 teaspoon vanilla extract

Directions:
1. In a blender, place the strawberries, apple juice, lemon juice, honey, and vanilla extract and blend until smooth.
2. Pour the mixture into 7 Popsicle molds and freeze for 4 hours or overnight. Enjoy!

Nutrition Info:
- Per Serving: Calories: 41 ; Fat: 0 g ;Saturated fat: 0g ;Sodium: 2 mg

Peach Melba Frozen Yogurt Parfaits

Servings: 4
Cooking Time: 5 Minutes
Ingredients:

- 2 tablespoons slivered almonds
- 1 tablespoon brown sugar
- 2 peaches, peeled and chopped (see Ingredient Tip)
- 1 cup fresh raspberries
- 2 cups no-sugar-added vanilla frozen yogurt
- 2 tablespoons peach jam
- 2 tablespoons raspberry jam or preserves

Directions:

1. In a small nonstick skillet over medium heat, combine the almonds and brown sugar.
2. Cook, stirring frequently, until the sugar melts and coats the almonds, about 3 to 4 minutes. Remove from the heat and put the almonds on a plate to cool.
3. To make the parfaits: In four parfait or wine glasses, layer each with the peaches, raspberries, frozen yogurt, peach jam, and raspberry jam. Top each glass with the caramelized almonds.

Nutrition Info:

- Per Serving: Calories: 263 ; Fat: 5 g ;Saturated fat: 1 g ;Sodium: 91 mg

Chocolate Granola Pie

Servings: 12
Ingredients:

- 3 tablespoons butter or margarine
- 2 (1-ounce) squares unsweetened chocolate, chopped
- ¼ cup brown sugar
- ½ cup dark corn syrup
- 2 teaspoons vanilla
- 1 egg
- 3 egg whites
- 2 cups Cinnamon Granola
- 1 Loco Pie Crust , unbaked

Directions:

1. Preheat oven to 350ºF. In large saucepan, combine butter and chocolate. Melt over low heat, stirring frequently, until smooth. Remove from heat and add brown sugar, corn syrup, vanilla, egg, and egg whites and beat well until blended.
2. Stir in granola and pour into pie crust. Bake for 40–50 minutes or until filling is set and pie crust is deep golden brown. Let cool completely and serve.

Nutrition Info:

- Per Serving: Calories: 384.56; Fat:14.45 g ;Saturated fat:4.65 g;Sodium:137.51 mg

Raisin Chocolate Slices

Servings: 16
Cooking Time: 30 Min

Ingredients:
- Cooking spray
- 2 cups raisins
- 3 large free-range eggs
- 1 cup whole-wheat flour
- ½ cup unsweetened cocoa powder
- ¼ cup sunflower oil
- 1 teaspoon baking soda
- Pinch fine sea salt

Directions:
1. Heat the oven to 350°F gas mark 4. Coat a deep baking dish with cooking spray, set aside.
2. Bring a small stockpot of water to the boil and remove from the heat.
3. In a medium-sized mixing bowl, cover the raisins with the boiling water, soak for 15 minutes, drain.
4. In a food processor, add the raisins and 2 tbsp. of water, process until smooth.
5. Add the eggs, one at a time, mixing between each addition.
6. Add the flour, cocoa powder, sunflower oil, baking soda, and salt, mix until well combined.
7. Pour the batter into the prepared baking dish and bake for 30 minutes, or until the toothpick inserted comes out clean.
8. Remove from the oven and cool completely.

Nutrition Info:
- Per Serving: Calories: 125; Fat: 7 g ;Saturated fat: 1 g ;Sodium: 103 mg

Loco Pie Crust

Servings: 8

Ingredients:
- ½ cup plus
- 1 tablespoon mayonnaise
- 3 tablespoons buttermilk
- 1 teaspoon vinegar
- 1½ cups flour

Directions:
1. In large bowl, combine mayonnaise, buttermilk, and vinegar and mix well. Add flour, stirring with a fork to form a ball. You may need to add more buttermilk or more flour to make a workable dough. Press dough into a ball, wrap in plastic wrap, and refrigerate for 1 hour.
2. When ready to bake, preheat oven to 400°F. Roll out dough between two sheets of waxed paper. Remove top sheet and place crust in 9″ pie pan. Carefully ease off the top sheet of paper, then ease the crust into the pan and press to bottom and sides. Fold edges under and flute.
3. Either use as recipe directs, or bake for 5 minutes, then press crust down with fork if necessary. Bake for 5–8 minutes longer or until crust is light golden brown.

Nutrition Info:
- Per Serving: Calories:171.83; Fat: 7.35 g ;Saturated fat:1.18 g;Sodium: 65.46 mg

Cinnamon And Walnut Baked Pears

Servings: 4
Cooking Time: 25 Minutes
Ingredients:

- 2 ripe Bosc pears, halved and cored
- ¼ teaspoon cinnamon
- 2 tablespoons crushed walnuts
- 2 teaspoons maple syrup

Directions:

1. Preheat the oven to 350°F. Line a baking sheet with parchment paper.
2. Place the pear halves on the prepared baking sheet, hollow-side up, and sprinkle with the cinnamon. Fill the hollow with the walnuts.
3. Bake the pears for 25 minutes.
4. Drizzle the pear halves with the maple syrup and enjoy immediately.

Nutrition Info:

- Per Serving: Calories: 171 ; Fat: 3g ;Saturated fat: 0g ;Sodium: 3mg

Mango Walnut Upside-down Cake

Servings: 12
Ingredients:

- 2 tablespoons plus
- ¼ cup butter, divided
- ¼ cup dark brown sugar
- ¼ teaspoon cardamom
- ½ teaspoon cinnamon
- 1 mango, peeled and sliced
- ¼ cup vegetable oil
- ½ cup sugar
- ½ cup brown sugar
- 2 egg whites
- 1 egg
- ¼ cup yogurt
- ¼ cup orange juice
- 1 teaspoon baking powder
- 1 teaspoon baking soda
- 1½ cups flour
- ½ cup whole-wheat flour

Directions:

1. Preheat oven to 350°F. Spray a 12-cup Bundt pan with nonstick baking spray containing flour and set aside. In small microwave-safe bowl, combine 2 tablespoons butter with dark brown sugar. Microwave on high for 1 minute until butter melts; stir until smooth. Add cardamom and cinnamon.
2. Spoon this mixture into prepared pan. Arrange mango slices on top; set aside.
3. In large bowl, combine ¼ cup butter, oil, sugar, and brown sugar and beat until smooth. Add egg whites and egg and beat well. Add yogurt and orange juice, then baking powder, baking soda, flour, and whole-wheat flour. Beat for 1 minute.
4. Pour batter over mangoes in pan. Bake for 50–60 minutes or until a toothpick inserted in cake comes out clean. Let cool for 5 minutes, then invert onto serving tray. If any mango mixture remains in pan, spoon over cake. Let cool completely.

Choc Chip Banana Muffins

Servings: 8
Cooking Time: 20 Min
Ingredients:
- 2 tbsp. ground flaxseeds
- 5 tbsp. water
- 2 cups almond flour
- 1 tbsp. ground cinnamon
- 1 tsp baking powder
- 3 (1 cup) medium ripe bananas, mashed
- 2 tbsp. organic honey
- ¼ cup dark chocolate chips
- 1 tsp vanilla extract
- ¼ cup unsalted walnuts, chopped

Directions:
1. Heat the oven to 375°F gas mark 5. Line a muffin tin with 8 muffin cup liners. Set aside.
2. In a small-sized mixing bowl, stir in the flaxseeds and water and let this sit for 5 minutes until the mixture congeals.
3. In a large-sized mixing bowl, add the almond flour, cinnamon, and baking powder and mix to combine.
4. In a medium-sized mixing bowl, add the flaxseed mixture, bananas, honey, chocolate chips, and vanilla extract, mix to combine. Slowly pour the wet ingredients into the dry ingredients, mix well. Add in the walnuts and mix.
5. Spoon the mixture evenly into the 8 lined muffin tin, bake for 20 minutes, or until the inserted toothpick comes out clean.
6. Serve warm or once completely cooled, store in an airtight container to stay fresh.

Nutrition Info:
- Per Serving: Calories: 199 ; Fat: 5 g ;Saturated fat: 1 g ;Sodium: 64 mg

Sweet Potato And Chocolate Muffins

Servings: 12
Cooking Time: 25 Minutes
Ingredients:
- ¾ cup mashed, cooked sweet potato
- ½ cup soy milk
- ½ cup brown sugar
- ⅓ cup canola oil
- 2 large eggs
- 1¾ cups whole-wheat flour
- ¾ cup rolled oats
- 1½ teaspoons baking powder
- ¾ teaspoon baking soda
- ¼ teaspoon ground cinnamon
- ¼ teaspoon ground nutmeg
- ½ cup mini dark chocolate chips

Directions:
1. Preheat the oven to 350°F.
2. Line 12 muffin cups with paper liners and set aside.

3. In a medium bowl, whisk together the sweet potato, soy milk, brown sugar, canola oil, and eggs until well blended.
4. In a large bowl, stir together the flour, oats, baking powder, baking soda, cinnamon, nutmeg, and chocolate chips.
5. Add the wet ingredients to the dry ingredients and stir until just combined. Spoon the batter into the prepared muffin cups, filling each cup about two-thirds full.
6. Place the muffins in the oven and bake until a toothpick inserted in the center comes out clean, about 25 minutes.
7. Store in an airtight container in the refrigerator for up to 5 days, or freeze for up to 3 months.

Nutrition Info:
- Per Serving: Calories: 242 ; Fat: 10 g ;Saturated fat: 3 g ;Sodium: 104 mg

Loaded Soy Yogurt Bowls

Servings: X
Ingredients:
- 2 cups unsweetened vanilla soy yogurt
- 1 banana, sliced
- ½ cup raspberries or blueberries
- ¼ cup chopped pistachios
- ¼ cup roasted unsalted sunflower seeds
- 2 tablespoons honey
- 1 tablespoon hemp hearts, for garnish
- 1 tablespoon cacao nibs, for garnish

Directions:
1. Divide the yogurt between two bowls.
2. Evenly divide the banana, berries, pistachios, and sunflower seeds between the bowls.
3. Drizzle each bowl with 1 tablespoon of honey and top them with hemp hearts and cacao nibs.
4. Serve.

Nutrition Info:
- Per Serving: Calories: 394 ; Fat: 18 g ;Saturated fat: 2 g ;Sodium: 57 mg

Chocolate Chia Pudding

Servings: 2
Cooking Time: 4 Hours
Ingredients:
- 1 cup low-fat milk
- ½ cup chia seeds
- 2 tablespoons cocoa powder
- 1 tablespoon maple syrup
- 1 tablespoon vanilla extract

Directions:
1. In a small bowl, combine the milk, chia seeds, cocoa powder, maple syrup, and vanilla extract.
2. Let the mixture stand for 10 to 15 minutes, stir again, and divide it between 2 Mason jars or lidded containers. Seal and refrigerate for 4 hours or overnight.

Nutrition Info:
- Per Serving: Calories:383 ; Fat: 19g ;Saturated fat: 3g ;Sodium: 66mg

Luscious Mocha Mousse

Servings: X
Cooking Time: 10 Minutes
Ingredients:
- 4 ounces 70-percent dark chocolate, finely chopped
- ¾ cup unsweetened soy milk
- ½ teaspoon espresso powder
- ½ teaspoon pure vanilla extract
- Pinch sea salt
- 4 ounces silken tofu, drained well

Directions:
1. Place the chocolate in a medium bowl and set aside.
2. In a small saucepan, warm the soy milk, espresso powder, vanilla, and salt over medium-high heat.
3. Bring the mixture to a boil and then pour it over the chocolate. Let the mixture stand for 10 minutes, then whisk until the chocolate is completely melted and the mixture is blended.
4. Pour the chocolate mixture into a food processor or blender and add the tofu. Pulse until very smooth.
5. Spoon the mousse into two bowls and refrigerate until firm, about 2 hours.
6. Serve.

Nutrition Info:
- Per Serving: Calories: 441 ; Fat: 38 g ;Saturated fat: 21 g ;Sodium: 213 mg

Apple Cheesecake

Servings: 2
Cooking Time: 25 Min
Ingredients:
- Aluminum foil
- 2 small honey crisp apples, cut in half and core removed
- 1 tsp coconut oil, melted
- 2 tbsp. organic honey, divided
- ⅛ tsp ground cinnamon
- ¼ cup fat-free cream cheese
- ⅛ tsp vanilla extract
- 2 tbsp. walnuts, chopped for garnish

Directions:
1. Heat the oven to 400°F gas mark 6.
2. Line a baking sheet with aluminum foil and arrange the apple halves on the sheet, cut side up.
3. Brush the cut side of the apples with coconut oil. Drizzle 1 tbsp. honey and sprinkle the cinnamon over the apple halves. Bake for 15 minutes.
4. While the apples are baking, in a small-sized mixing bowl, add the cream cheese, remaining 1 tbsp. organic honey, and vanilla extract, mix until well blended.
5. Divide the cream cheese mixture among the apple halves and bake for 10 minutes.
6. Garnish with walnuts and serve.

Nutrition Info:
- Per Serving: Calories: 307 ; Fat: 16g;Saturated fat: 7 g ;Sodium: 90 mg

Strawberry-mango Meringue Pie

Servings: 8

Ingredients:

- 1 teaspoon flour
- 3 egg whites
- ¼ teaspoon cream of tartar
- ½ cup sugar
- 1 teaspoon vanilla
- 1 (8-ounce) package low-fat cream cheese, softened
- 1 cup mango yogurt
- 1 cup chopped strawberries
- 2 mangoes, peeled and chopped

Directions:

1. Preheat oven to 300ºF. Spray a 9″ pie plate with nonstick cooking spray and dust with 1 teaspoon flour. In large bowl, combine egg whites and cream of tartar; beat until soft peaks form. Gradually beat in sugar until very stiff peaks form. Beat in vanilla. Spread into prepared pan, building up sides to form a shell.
2. Bake for 50–60 minutes or until shell is very light golden and dry to the touch. Turn oven off and let shell stand in oven for 1 hour. Cool completely.
3. For filling, in medium bowl beat cream cheese until fluffy. Gradually add yogurt, beating until well combined. Fold in strawberries and mangoes. Spoon into meringue pie shell, cover, and chill for 3–4 hours before serving.

Nutrition Info:

- Per Serving: Calories: 195.15; Fat:5.51 g ;Saturated fat: 3.40 g;Sodium:123.32 mg

Chocolate Mousse Banana Meringue Pie

Servings: 8

Ingredients:

- 1 recipe meringue pie shell
- 3 tablespoons cocoa powder
- 1 recipe Silken Chocolate Mousse
- 2 bananas, sliced
- 1 tablespoon lemon juice

Directions:

1. Follow directions to make meringue pie shell, but also beat cocoa into egg whites along with the sugar. Bake as directed in recipe. Let cool completely.
2. Make mousse as directed and chill in bowl for 4–6 hours until firm. Slice bananas, sprinkling lemon juice over slices as you work.
3. Layer mousse and sliced bananas in pie shell, beginning and ending with mousse. Cover and chill for 2–3 hours before serving.

Nutrition Info:

- Per Serving: Calories: 253.53; Fat:9.23 g ;Saturated fat: 5.94 g;Sodium:79.66 mg

Whole-wheat Chocolate Chip Cookies

Servings: 48

Ingredients:

- ¼ cup butter or plant sterol margarine, softened
- 1½ cups brown sugar
- ½ cup applesauce
- 1 tablespoon vanilla
- 1 egg
- 2 egg whites
- 2½ cups whole-wheat pastry flour
- ½ cup ground oatmeal
- 1 teaspoon baking soda
- ¼ teaspoon salt
- 2 cups special dark chocolate chips
- 1 cup chopped hazelnuts

Directions:

1. Preheat oven to 375°F. Line cookie sheets with parchment paper or Sil-pat silicone liners and set aside.
2. In large bowl, combine butter, brown sugar, and applesauce and beat well until smooth. Add vanilla, egg, and egg whites and beat until combined.
3. Add flour, oatmeal, baking soda, and salt and mix until a dough forms. Fold in chocolate chips and hazelnuts.
4. Drop dough by rounded teaspoons onto prepared cookie sheets. Bake for 7–10 minutes or until cookies are light golden brown and set. Let cool for 5 minutes before removing from cookie sheet to wire rack to cool.

Nutrition Info:

- Per Serving: Calories: 114.86; Fat:4.89 g ;Saturated fat:2.04 g;Sodium:26.49 mg

Curried Fruit Compote

Servings: 6
Cooking Time: 10 Minutes

Ingredients:

- 1 (8-ounce) can pineapple chunks, undrained
- 1 ripe pear, peeled and chopped
- 1 Granny Smith apple, chopped
- ⅓ cup dried cranberries
- 1 cup apple juice
- 1 tablespoon fresh lemon juice
- 2 tablespoons agave nectar or packed brown sugar
- 1 tablespoon curry powder
- 1 tablespoon cornstarch
- Pinch salt

Directions:

1. In a medium saucepan over medium heat, combine the pineapple chunks, pear, apple, cranberries, apple juice, lemon juice, agave nectar (or brown sugar), curry powder, cornstarch, and salt. Stir to blend.
2. Bring to a boil, reduce the heat to low, and simmer for 6 to 8 minutes or until the fruit is tender.
3. At this point, you can serve the compote as-is, or you can purée all—or part—of it. The compote can be stored in the refrigerator for up to 3 days. You can rewarm the compote on the stovetop before you serve it.

Nutrition Info:

- Per Serving: Calories: 112 ; Fat: 0 g ;Saturated fat: 0 g ;Sodium: 4 mg

Chocolate, Peanut Butter, And Banana Ice Cream

Servings: 2
Ingredients:

- 2 frozen bananas, peeled and sliced
- 2 tablespoons cocoa powder
- 1 tablespoon honey
- 2 tablespoons all-natural peanut butter
- 1 tablespoon chopped walnuts (or nut of choice)

Directions:

1. Put the frozen bananas, cocoa powder, honey, and peanut butter into a high-speed blender and blend until smooth.
2. Transfer the ice cream mixture into a resealable container and freeze for 2 hours.
3. Once frozen, scoop the ice cream into two serving bowls and top with walnuts.

Nutrition Info:

- Per Serving: Calories: 269 ; Fat: 12 g ;Saturated fat: 2 g ;Sodium: 5 mg

Fudge Brownies

Servings: 6
Cooking Time: 15 Min
Ingredients:

- 12 tsp raisins
- 1½ oz 80% dark chocolate bar, roughly chopped
- 2 tbsp. instant oatmeal
- 2 tbsp. unsweetened cocoa powder
- 2 tbsp. unsalted cashew butter
- 2 tbsp. water

Directions:

1. Heat the oven to 350°F gas mark 4.
2. In a food processor, add the black beans, raisins, chocolate, oatmeal, cocoa powder, cashew butter, and water. Blend for 2 to 3 minutes until smooth and doughy.
3. Pour the batter into an 8-inch square baking pan and spread evenly. Bake for 15 minutes, or until the inserted toothpick comes out clean.
4. Allow to cool for 5 minutes before cutting into 6 squares. Store in an airtight container to keep it fresh.

Nutrition Info:

- Per Serving: Calories: 160 ; Fat: 6 g ;Saturated fat:2 g ;Sodium: 3 mg

4-Week Meal Plan

Week 1

	Breakfast		Lunch		Dinner	
Day 1	Nutty Oat Cereal	13	Red Wine Chicken	24	Cod Satay	50
Day 2	Tempeh Caprese Breakfast Sandwiches	18	Beef Rollups With Pesto	37	Salmon With Farro Pilaf	51
Day 3	Carrot-oatmeal Bread	22	Halibut Parcels	49	Peanut-butter-banana Skewered Sammies	61
Day 4	Cashew & Berry Shake	15	Pork Quesadillas	37	Salad Sandwich	63
Day 5	Spinach Artichoke Pizza	15	Classic Spaghetti And Meatballs	38	Chili-sautéed Tofu With Almonds	64
Day 6	Honey-wheat Sesame Bread	21	Steamed Sole Rolls With Greens	51	Rice-and-vegetable Casserole	65
Day 7	Spicy Omelet	12	Pork Scallops Françoise	39	Bean And Veggie Cassoulet	64

Week 2

	Breakfast		Lunch		Dinner	
Day 1	Ciabatta Rolls	13	Turkey Tacos Verde	25	Pinto Bean Tortillas	65
Day 2	Egg White And Avocado Breakfast Wrap	18	Spinach And Kale Salad With Spicy Pork	36	Red Snapper With Fruit Salsa	59
Day 3	Tempeh Caprese Breakfast Sandwiches	18	Cowboy Steak With Chimichurri Sauce	38	Salad Sandwich	63
Day 4	Moroccan Lamb Kabobs	12	Salmon With Farro Pilaf	51	Quinoa-stuffed Peppers	66
Day 5	Rolled Oats Cereal	19	Tilapia Mint Wraps	52	Fennel-and-orange Salad	73
Day 6	Fruity Oatmeal Coffee Cake	20	Beef And Avocado Quesadillas	39	Tandoori Turkey Pizzas	33
Day 7	Blueberry-walnut Muffins	16	Chops With Mint And Garlic	49	Cashew Chicken	32

Week 3

	Breakfast		Lunch		Dinner	
Day 1	Corn-and-chili Pancakes	68	Cod And Potatoes	53	Fiery Pork Stir-fry	47
Day 2	Honey-wheat Sesame Bread	21	Pork Goulash	40	Turkey Curry With Fruit	31
Day 3	Cranberry-orange Bread	20	Catalán Salmon Tacos	54	Hearty Vegetable Stew	66
Day 4	Greek Quesadillas	78	Sesame-crusted Chicken	26	Spaghetti Sauce	67
Day 5	Oven-baked French Toast	14	Beef Burrito Skillet	41	Tandoori Turkey Pizzas	33
Day 6	Banana Oat Pancakes	14	Chicken Spicy Thai Style	26	Corned-beef Hash	46
Day 7	Orange-vanilla Smoothie	16	Sirloin Meatballs In Sauce	42	Stuffed Noodle Squash	67

Week 4

	Breakfast		Lunch		Dinner	
Day 1	Sweet Potato And Chocolate Muffins	98	Citrus Cod Bake	53	Quinoa Pepper Pilaf	68
Day 2	Pinto Bean Tortillas	65	Pork Scallops With Spinach	41	Almond Snapper With Shrimp Sauce	58
Day 3	Chocolate Granola Pie	95	Sliced Flank Steak With Sherry-mustard Sauce	44	Roasted Shrimp And Veggies	54
Day 4	Strawberry-mango Meringue Pie	101	Cabbage Roll Sauté	44	Kidney Bean Stew	70
Day 5	Choc Chip Banana Muffins	98	Cajun-rubbed Fish	56	Sesame Soba Noodles	70
Day 6	Orange-vanilla Smoothie	16	Chicken Breasts With Salsa	33	Pumpkin And Chickpea Patties	71
Day 7	Blueberry-banana Smoothie	17	Baked Halibut In Mustard Sauce	56	Basil Chicken Meatballs	29

APPENDIX : Recipes Index

A

Almond Snapper With Shrimp Sauce 58

Apple Cheesecake 100

Avocado And Kiwi Green Smoothies 19

Avocado Dressing 91

B

Baked Halibut In Mustard Sauce 56

Balsamic Blueberry Chicken 31

Banana Oat Pancakes 14

Banana-rum Mousse 94

Basil Chicken Meatballs 29

Bean And Veggie Cassoulet 64

Beans For Soup 78

Beef And Avocado Quesadillas 39

Beef Burrito Skillet 41

Beef Rollups With Pesto 37

Blueberry-banana Smoothie 17

Blueberry-walnut Muffins 16

Bluefish With Asian Seasonings 59

butternut Squash And Lentil Soup 75

C

Cabbage Roll Sauté 44

Cajun-rubbed Fish 56

Carrot-oatmeal Bread 22

Cashew & Berry Shake 15

Cashew Chicken 32

Catalán Salmon Tacos 54

Cauliflower, Green Pea, And Wild Rice Pilaf 69

Cheese-and-veggie Stuffed Artichokes 62

Cheesy Spinach Dip 90

Chicken Breasts With Mashed Beans 30

Chicken Breasts With Salsa 33

Chicken Pesto 27

Chicken Spicy Thai Style 26

Chicken Stir-fry With Napa Cabbage 24

Chili Fries 82

Chili-sautéed Tofu With Almonds 64

Chimichurri Rub 85

Chimichurri Sauce 88

Choc Chip Banana Muffins 98

Chocolate Chia Pudding 99

Chocolate Granola Pie 95

Chocolate Mousse Banana Meringue Pie 101

Chocolate, Peanut Butter, And Banana Ice Cream 103

Chops With Mint And Garlic 40

Chunky Irish Potato-leek Soup 81

Ciabatta Rolls 13

Cinnamon And Walnut Baked Pears 97

Citrus Cod Bake 53

Classic Italian Tomato Sauce 91

Classic Spaghetti And Meatballs 38

Cod And Potatoes 53

Cod Satay 50

Corn-and-chili Pancakes 68

Corned-beef Hash 46

Cosmoked Salmon And Turkey Wasabi Wraps 73

Cowboy Steak With Chimichurri Sauce 38

Cranberry-orange Bread 20

Crunchy Chicken Coleslaw Salad 29

Curried Fruit Compote 102

D

Double Tomato Sauce 86

E

Egg White And Avocado Breakfast Wrap 18

F

Fennel-and-orange Salad 73

Fiery Pork Stir-fry 47

Fresh Lime Salsa 84

Fruity Oatmeal Coffee Cake 20

Fudge Brownies 103

G

Good-morning Muffins 17

Greek Quesadillas 78

Green Sauce 86

Grilled Scallops With Gremolata 49

Grilled Vegetable Pasta Salad 76

H

Halibut Burgers 52

Halibut Parcels 49

Hearty Vegetable Stew 66

Homestyle Bean Soup 61

Honey-wheat Sesame Bread 21

Hot-and-spicy Peanut Thighs 27

K

Kidney Bean Stew 70

L

Legume Chili 80

Lemon Basil Pork Medallions 42

Lemon-garlic Sauce 92

Lemony Green Beans With Almonds 75

Loaded Soy Yogurt Bowls 99

Loco Pie Crust 96

Low-sodium Chicken Broth 81

Luscious Mocha Mousse 100

M

Mango Walnut Upside-down Cake 97

Maple-balsamic Pork Chops 43

Mini Turkey Meatloaves 28

Moroccan Lamb Kabobs 12

Mustard And Thyme–crusted Beef Tenderloin 45

Mustard Berry Vinaigrette 89

Mustard-roasted Almond Chicken Tenders 28

N

Nutty Coconut Chicken With Fruit Sauce 32

Nutty Oat Cereal 13

O

Orange-vanilla Smoothie 16

Oregano-thyme Sauce 88

Oven-baked French Toast 14

P

Peach Melba Frozen Yogurt Parfaits 95

Peanut-butter-banana Skewered Sammies 61

Pinto Bean Tortillas 65

Piquant Navy Beans 74

Pork Chops With Cabbage 45

Pork Goulash 40

Pork Quesadillas 37

Pork Scallops Françoise 39

Pork Scallops With Spinach 41

Pumpkin And Chickpea Patties 71

Q

Quinoa Pepper Pilaf 68

Quinoa-stuffed Peppers 66

R

Raisin Chocolate Slices 96

Red Snapper With Fruit Salsa 59

Red Wine Chicken 24

Rice-and-vegetable Casserole 65

Roasted Garlic Soufflé 62

Roasted Shrimp And Veggies 54

Roasted-garlic Corn 76

Rocket & Goat Cheese 77

Rolled Oats Cereal 19

S

Salad Sandwich 63

Salmon With Farro Pilaf 51

Salmon With Spicy Mixed Beans 57

Sautéed Chicken With Roasted Garlic Sauce 34

Sautéed Fennel With Lemon 77

Scalloped Potatoes With Aromatic Vegetables 79

Scallops On Skewers With Lemon 58

Seared Scallops With Fruit 57

Sesame Soba Noodles 70

Sesame-crusted Chicken 26

Sesame-pepper Salmon Kabobs 55

Sesame-roasted Vegetables 80

Silken Fruited Tofu Cream 84

Sirloin Meatballs In Sauce 42

Sliced Flank Steak With Sherry-mustard Sauce 44

Smoky Barbecue Rub 85

Spaghetti Sauce 67

Spaghetti With Creamy Tomato Sauce 63

Spicy Honey Sauce 92

Spicy Omelet 12

Spicy Peanut Sauce 90

Spinach And Kale Salad With Spicy Pork 36

Spinach And Walnut Pesto 92

Spinach Artichoke Pizza 15

Spring Asparagus Soup 82

Steamed Sole Rolls With Greens 51

Strawberry-apple-lemon Smoothie Pops 94

Strawberry-mango Meringue Pie 101

Stuffed Noodle Squash 67

Sun-dried Tomato And Kalamata Olive Tapenade 87

Sweet Potato And Chocolate Muffins 98

T

Tandoori Turkey Pizzas 33

Tangy Fish And Tofu Soup 79

Tempeh Caprese Breakfast Sandwiches 18

Tilapia Mint Wraps 52

Tofu-horseradish Sauce 89

Turkey Breast With Dried Fruit 25

Turkey Curry With Fruit 31

Turkey Tacos Verde 25

Tzatziki 88

W

Whole-wheat Chocolate Chip Cookies 102

Y

Yogurt Cheese Balls 74

Z

Zesty Citrus Kefir Dressing 87

Printed in Great Britain
by Amazon

40262873R00064